● When you hear a **k** sound at the end of a syllable or word, the letters **k, ck,** or **que** will usually stand for that sound.

Letters	Examples	Sound
k	kangaroo	/k/
ck	pickle	/k/
que	clique	/k/

Directions: Use one of the phrases below to answer each question. Then circle the letters in each answer that make the /k/ sound.

a sneak peek   **a unique antique**   **a trick brick**

1. What could you call something that is very old and very unusual? _____

2. What could you call a piece of fake building material? _____

3. What would you call it if you got a glimpse of your birthday present while it was still

   hidden in the closet? _____

Directions: Fourteen words containing **k, ck,** or **que** are hidden in the puzzle below. Some go across, and others go up and down. Circle each word as you find it in the puzzle, then copy the word under the correct heading.

k words   **ck** words

_____   _____   _____   _____

_____

_____

_____

_____

que words

_____

_____

```
K  H  B  Z  T  R  I  C  K  P  C  S
E  K  O  R  Q  K  E  Y  N  P  B  T
P  S  U  A  U  R  A  K  E  E  X  U
T  V  T  L  O  O  K  Z  S  T  U  C
Q  U  I  C  K  M  C  I  S  A  C  K
S  U  Q  T  E  C  H  N  I  Q  U  E
L  K  U  Q  L  G  X  W  C  H  V  Y
E  I  E  X  U  F  C  E  K  I  T  E
E  U  B  C  C  J  K  D  C  K  D  D
K  L  N  O  K  E  T  T  L  E  J  K
```

● **Qu** stands for the sound /kw/.

Letters	Examples	Sounds
qu	queen	/kw/
kn	knee	/n/

Directions: Write each word beside its definition.

quest   questionnaire   queen
quicksand   quarterback

1. a female monarch _____

2. a journey in search of adventure _____

3. the football player who usually calls the signals _____

4. a written form used for gathering information _____

5. wet, loose, deep sand into which a person can sink _____

● When **k** comes before **n** it is not sounded. **Kn** stands for the /n/ sound.

Directions: Put each group of words in order so that they make a sentence. Remember to begin the first word of each sentence with a capital letter. Then end the sentence with a period.

1. knows how Nelson knit to

    _____

2. ceremony knight during the knelt the

    _____

3. Pat's joint was out of knee knocked

    _____

● **Ch** usually stands for the sound you hear at the beginning and end of **church.** But sometimes **ch** can stand for the /k/ or /sh/ sounds.

Letters	Examples	Sounds
ch	character	/k/
ch	cheap	/ch/
ch	chauffeur	/sh/

Directions: Read each sentence. Circle the word in each sentence that contains a **ch.** Then circle the sound that **ch** stands for in that word.

1.	The orchestra is practicing a concerto.	/k/	/ch/	/sh/
2.	The chandelier sparkled in the sunlight.	/k/	/ch/	/sh/
3.	Lee read the last three chapters of the book last night.	/k/	/ch/	/sh/
4.	Jean is learning to play chess.	/k/	/ch/	/sh/
5.	The mechanic put a new muffler on the car.	/k/	/ch/	/sh/
6.	His toe aches when it is going to rain.	/k/	/ch/	/sh/
7.	The limbs of the tree etched a lacy pattern against the sky.	/k/	/ch/	/sh/
8.	Greg is saving his allowance to purchase a new bike.	/k/	/ch/	/sh/
9.	Her brother is studying architecture in college.	/k/	/ch/	/sh/
10.	Does your little sister go to school yet?	/k/	/ch/	/sh/
11.	Do you think chives taste like onions?	/k/	/ch/	/sh/
12.	When Sue yelled into the canyon, she heard an echo.	/k/	/ch/	/sh/
13.	My uncle is a chef in Toronto.	/k/	/ch/	/sh/
14.	Branches grow very quickly on willow trees.	/k/	/ch/	/sh/
15.	We have the best teacher in the world.	/k/	/ch/	/sh/
16.	Which one of the twins was there?	/k/	/ch/	/sh/
17.	The mother cat carried each of her kittens back to the box.	/k/	/ch/	/sh/

3

● The letter **c** usually stands for the hard sound /k/ when it comes before **a, o,** or **u.**
C usually stands for the soft sound /s/ when it comes before **e, i,** or **y.**

Letter	Examples	Sounds
c	camp	/k/
c	race	/s/

Directions: As you read the following story, circle each word that contains a **c.** Write each word you circled in the correct column. Use each word only once.

In 1492, Columbus didn't only discover America. He also found that the Indians were cultivating a strange, grasslike plant that today is one of the four most valuable crops grown in the entire world—corn.

Of course, the North American Indians had been growing corn for countless decades. Corn played an important part in their everyday life. Indians held ceremonies when placing the seeds in the soil. They used corn patterns to decorate ceramic pottery and sculpture.

Early colonists enjoyed juicy ears of corn on the cob and hot, buttered popcorn. Corn was so valuable to the colonists that they often used it as money. People paid their rent, taxes, or debts in corn. They even traded it for marriage licenses!

c sounded as /k/ _____ **c** sounded as /s/

_____ _____ _____

_____ _____ _____

_____ _____ _____

_____ _____ _____

_____ _____ _____

_____ _____

4

● **G** usually stands for the hard sound in **gate** when it comes before **a, o,** or **u.** The letter **g** usually stands for the soft sound /j/ when it comes before **e, i,** or **y.**

Letter	Examples	Sounds
g	game	/g/
g	page	/j/

Directions: Read each word. If you don't recognize it, look up the word in your dictionary. Write **/g/** on the line if the word has the hard sound of **g.** Write **/j/** on the line if the word has the soft sound of **g.**

gymnast _____   gleeful _____   gazebo _____   galloping _____

arrangement _____   gym _____   rage _____   sponge _____

region _____   guess _____   age _____   tragedy _____

Directions: Use the words in the exercise above to solve the crossword puzzle.

Across

4. a disaster or serious event
5. a summerhouse from which one can gaze at the scenery
6. anger
7. moving very fast on a horse
9. an expert in gymnastics
11. number of years a person has lived

Down

1. the way in which something is put together or shown
2. a part of the earth's surface
3. joyful
8. give an estimate
10. something full of holes, used for cleaning

Directions: Circle each word that contains **g** in the sentences below. Then write each circled word in the correct column.

1. Sauerkraut and sausage make a spicy meal.
2. Our principal was glad to arrange the paper drive.
3. The jade earring dangled dangerously from the edge of the table.
4. The giant gourds Angie grew will be sold at the grocery store.
5. Sandy giggled at the outrageous joke.
6. Glucose is another name for the sugar in fruits and honey.
7. The giant flying saucer cast a ghostly glow as it landed on the ground.
8. The secret agent was disguised as a gardener.
9. Mr. and Mrs. Morgan are gracious people.
10. Gerry was the last passenger to board the big jet.

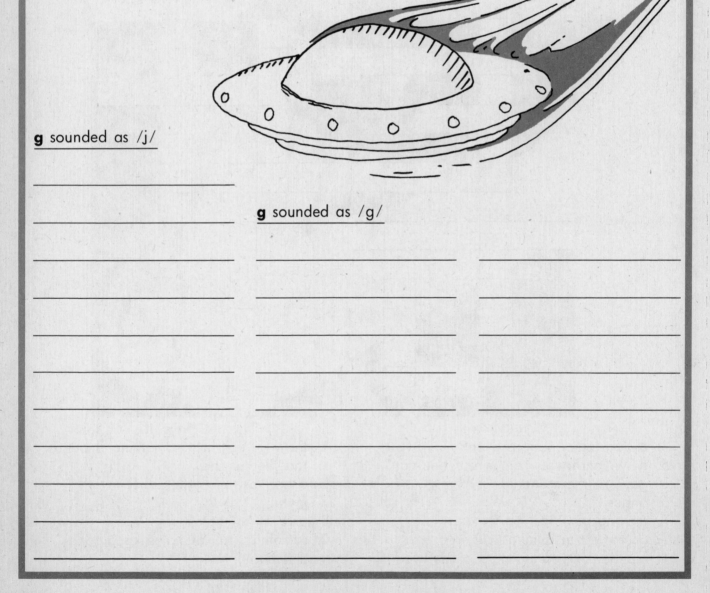

g sounded as /j/

_____

_____

g sounded as /g/

_____   _____

_____   _____

_____   _____

_____   _____

_____   _____

_____   _____

_____   _____

Directions: Read the list of words. Then read through the story. Write the correct word from the list on the line to complete each unfinished sentence. Remember to use your dictionary to check unfamiliar words.

marketplace   techniques
circle   knows
investigating   mystique
gigantic   questions
archaeologists   unlock

MYSTERY IN STONE

Ghostly giants tower over the Salisbury Plain in England. The huge stones have stood in this spot for over four thousand years—long before even the invention of the wheel.

People have been _____ Stonehenge for centuries, trying to
                          1

_____ its secrets. _____ are scientists who study
    2   3

ancient times and people. They have tried to find out what _____
                                                      4

Stonehenge's builders used to move the five-ton stones over one hundred miles to get them to Stonehenge.

Nobody _____ for sure why Stonehenge was built. Some people
                  5

think that it was a temple. Others think that Stonehenge may have been a graveyard, a

_____, or even a _____ calendar!
    6   7

Scientists and scholars from all over the world have been fascinated by the

_____ surrounding these ancient stones, but the few answers that they
    8

find only lead to more _____. Meanwhile, the great
                             9

_____ of stones stands silent, casting long shadows across the empty
    10

plain.

7

Directions: Suppose you are an archaeologist investigating Stonehenge. Decide which of the following techniques you would use to try and solve its mysteries. Put a check on the line in front of each one you choose.

_____ dig into the earth to find a clue

_____ study how the stones are put together

_____ stay there overnight with my friends

_____ forget what other scientists have found out

_____ study about the early people who lived on the Salisbury Plain

_____ read about all the legends of Stonehenge

_____ _____

(my idea)

Directions: Now tell about your way to solve the Stonehenge mystery. Finish the sentences that are started for you to explain the technique you would try.

Here's how I plan to solve the mystery of Stonehenge.

First, I'll _____

because _____.

Then I'll _____.

Finally, if that doesn't work, I'll solve the mystery by _____

_____.

8

● The letters **f, ff,** or **ph** can stand for the sound of /f/.

Letters	Examples	Sound
ph	dolphin	/f/
f	faster	/f/
ff	scaffold	/f/

Directions: Read the sentences. Circle the letter or letters that stand for the /f/ sound in each word in dark print. Then circle the answer to the question about that word.

1. Fred waters his **philodendron** twice a week.

   What is a **philodendron?**

   a car   a sweater   a plant

2. The doctor tapped Kim's knee to test her **reflexes.**

   What are **reflexes?**

   colors   a kind of graph   automatic actions

3. The white cat looked like a **phantom** as it crouched on the tree limb in the dark.

   What is a **phantom?**

   a wrestler   an elk   a ghost

4. Mike got an A on the test. He was glad that he had studied **sufficiently.**

   What does **sufficiently** mean?

   enough   practiced   repeated

5. On her birthday, Mom got a **fragrant** bouquet of roses.

   What does **fragrant** mean?

   plaid   starched   sweet-smelling

6. Stacy looks beautiful in her class photo. She certainly is **photogenic.**

   What does **photogenic** mean?

   scary   a person that sleeps a lot   looks attractive in a photograph

7. Fairy tales and myths are **fictional** stories.

   What does **fictional** mean?

   made-up   horse stories   grandmotherly

8. Meg made sure the birthday present she asked her dad for was **affordable.**

   What does **affordable** mean?

   sent back to   in a store   could be paid for

Directions: Circle the letters that make the /f/ sound in each word in the list. Then write each word from the list beside its definition. Use your dictionary if you need to.

affirmed	phonics	fundamental
sufficient	profession	pamphlets
festivities	affable	phantom

_____ basic

_____ leaflets

_____ enough

_____ celebration or merry party

_____ pleasant and easy to talk to

_____ a job that requires advanced education

_____ declared firmly, or stated that something is true

_____ a method for learning to read words that involves learning the usual sound of letters or groups of letters

Directions: Choose the correct word from the list to complete each sentence. Write the word on the line.

1. Our neighbors, the Scotts, are a very _____ and friendly family.

2. The referee _____ that our team got the point.

3. Bob reads unfamiliar words by using the _____ rules he has learned.

4. Reading and writing are _____ skills.

5. The parade included a marching band and floats as part of the _____ .

6. The teaching _____ has many dedicated members.

7. The dense fog made the ship look like a _____ as it sailed silently through the harbor.

8. Thomas Paine wrote stirring patriotic _____ before the Revolutionary War.

9. Emily has earned _____ points to get a scouting merit badge.

● The consonant **s** can stand for the sound you hear at the beginning of **safe**. But sometimes **s** can stand for /z/, or for /sh/, or sometimes for /zh/.

Letter	Examples	Sounds
s	sunny	/s/
s	rose	/z/
s	sure	/sh/
s	pleasure	/zh/

Directions: Draw a line under each word in the sentences below that contains an **s**. Then write /s/, /z/, /sh/, or /zh/ above each word you underlined to show the sound that **s** makes in that word.

1. If you go to the tennis match, you will want to wear casual clothes.

2. Did you know that Beethoven composed several pieces of music after he lost his hearing?

3. His nose was rosy because he was exposed to the cold.

4. Chris carefully measured the ingredients as he made the soup.

5. I used the garden hose to water the daisies and the roses.

6. Saul reassured his cousin about riding the Ferris wheel.

7. There was thunderous applause at the end of the musical.

8. Sam seldom loses his composure when he gets asked for his autograph.

9. Tess seems to have a sixth sense about people she meets.

10. I'm sorry you didn't see the sunset on Thursday.

11. Successful people are usually hard workers.

12. Are you sure you chose the correct size?

13. Is it possible that Sue has mumps?

14. Les felt drowsy after his busy day.

15. Six kids wore crimson socks.

Directions: Circle the word that correctly completes each sentence. The correct word should have the same **s** sound as the word in dark print above the sentence.

pose
1. Ted thought the test was _____.   hard   easy   simple

measure
2. The pirate buried his _____.   treasure   gold   cash

sentence
3. Eating a good diet is _____.   logical   sensible   wise

missile
4. How many letters did you _____?   write   compose   send

such
5. The sound was unexpected and _____.   noisy   sudden   loud

sack
6. What did you _____?   advise   recommend   suggest

sure
7. After the earthquake the ground had a large
   _____.   crack   fissure   split

sum
8. How many coupons did you _____?   preserve   lose   save

reassure
9. Who is the author of that _____?   expression   saying   poem

miss
10. The weather looks _____.   rosy   promising   rainy

song
11. Do you know the visitor's _____?   topic   reason   purpose

applause
12. A person that spreads rumors is called a
    _____.   busybody   gossip   snoop

● The letters **wh** can stand for /h/ as in **whole** or for /hw/ as in **whale**.

Letters	Examples	Sounds
wh	whole	/h/
wh	whale	/hw/

Directions: Read the article. Circle each word containing **wh.** Then write each of those words in the correct column below. Write each word only once.

Did you know that the largest kind of animal that has ever lived is swimming somewhere in the earth's oceans? This animal, whose body length can reach 95 feet (29 meters) long, is the blue whale. This whale is heavier than an elephant and bigger than the largest prehistoric dinosaur we know about.

When scientists study these huge animals, they tell us that they are among the most fascinating animals anywhere on earth. For example, while these whales have excellent hearing, they have somewhat small ear openings and no real ears at all on the outside of their bodies. These animals who live in the water must breathe air to survive. This means that a blue whale keeps its whole body under water for quite awhile. But it must bring the top of its head to the surface regularly to breathe air.

wh sounded as /h/

_____   _____   _____

wh sounded as /hw/

_____   _____   _____

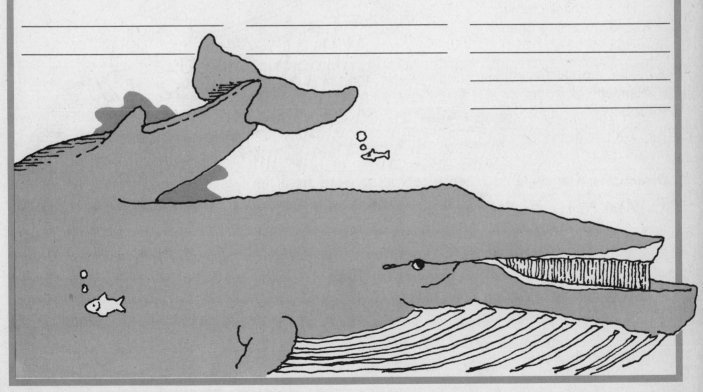

● The letters **sh, ci,** and **ti** can stand for /sh/ in words.

Letters	Examples	Sound
sh	ship	/sh/
ci	special	/sh/
ti	partial	/sh/

Directions: Read each pair of sentences. Underline each word in which you hear the /sh/ sound. Then circle the numeral of the sentence that describes the picture.

1. We sipped refreshments while we watched the accomplished magician.

2. The marshal was suspicious of the shrewd electrician.

1. Learning to be a computer technician takes special patience.

2. The beautician polished her stylish nails.

1. That bashful cashier is also an accomplished musician.

2. The shopper bought a shipment of artificial shrubbery.

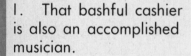

Directions: Complete each sentence with a word from the list.

1. Aunt Pam _____ the gift I gave her.   commercial

2. The weather in Alaska is often _____.   appreciated

3. The television _____ was about a new breakfast cereal.   shattered

4. Another word that means *enough* is _____.   harsh

5. The earthquake _____ the windows.   sufficient

Directions: Read the words in the list. Then read the paragraphs below. Write the word from the list that correctly completes each unfinished sentence.

profession	what	effort	physicians
Congressional	meanwhile	effective	someday
enough	raised	fight	office
disease	affect	leisure	

Jonas Salk was _____ in New York City. His father was a garment
                                    1

industry worker. But Jonas dreamed that _____ he would be part of the
                                          2

_____ of medicine. So he put a lot of _____ into his
            3   4

schoolwork. In his _____ time Jonas worked at part-time jobs to help
                          5

pay college expenses.

Finally, in 1939, Jonas Salk had received _____ education to
                                                    6

graduate from medical school. Instead of opening a doctor's _____, Salk
                                                                        7

chose to do research on viruses in a laboratory.

_____ a serious viral _____ was sweeping the
            8   9

country. Polio was a disease that many thousands of children between the ages of four

and fifteen contracted. Polio can _____ the nervous system and cause a
                                          10

person to lose the ability to move the arms and legs. Many _____ and
                                                                    11

parents were worried because polio epidemics were being reported.

For several years Salk worked patiently to develop a polio vaccine. Finally in 1953,

Salk announced that he had found _____ he had been looking for—a
                                          12

vaccine that would prevent polio. Salk, his wife and three children were among the first

volunteers to try the vaccine. The vaccine was found to be safe. It was then tested on

almost two million schoolchildren and is now used widely.

After years of effort, Jonas Salk was finally successful in the _____
                                                                        13

against polio.

15

Directions: Write the correct word or words from the list on page 15 to answer each question below.

1. In which word do the letters **ph** have the /f/ sound?

_____

2. In which word are letters **gh** not sounded?

_____

3. In which words do the letters **ff** have the /f/ sound?

_____ _____ _____ _____

● A **sentence** is a group of words that tells a complete thought or idea. Every sentence needs to have a subject and a verb. The subject tells who or what the sentence is about. The verb, or action word, tells what the subject is doing. The first word in the sentence begins with a capital letter. At the end of the sentence is a punctuation mark such as a period. Example: The Salk vaccine helps to prevent polio.

Directions: Think about an invention or discovery you would like to work on. Put a check next to the idea below that interests you or write your own idea.

_____ a new musical instrument   _____ a cure for a disease

_____ a faster, cheaper way to travel _____ a very speedy way to grow crops

_____ _____
(your idea)

Directions: Now use some of the words in the list below to help you answer the following questions about your invention or discovery. Use complete sentences.

unusual	effort	easy	everywhere	symphony
anywhere	might	enough	disease	research

1. What will your invention or discovery do or be used for?

_____

2. What tools will you need to work out your idea?

_____

3. Who are the people who would use and enjoy it?

_____

4. Why did you choose this item to invent or discover?

_____

● The letters **th** can stand for the sound /th/ you hear in **thin** or for the sound /th/ in **then**.

Directions: Write each word beside its definition. Then write **thin** or **then** to show the sound that **th** has in that word. Use your dictionary if you need to.

farther   marathon   clothes   authentic
worthy   enthusiastic   zenith   myth

Definition	word	sound of thin or then
eagerly interested	_____	_____
a long race or contest	_____	_____
coverings for the body	_____	_____
more far	_____	_____
something that is genuine or real	_____	_____
the highest point	_____	_____
something that has worth or merit	_____	_____
a legend or story about a made- up person or thing	_____	_____

Directions: Complete each sentence by choosing the correct word from the list at the top of the page.

1. Jan is very _____ about being chosen for the soccer team.

2. Bill can run _____ than Dan.

3. The story of Pegasus is a _____ about a flying horse.

4. When the firecracker reached its _____ , it exploded into beautiful colors.

5. The cave that we visited had some _____ paintings by cave dwellers.

6. My brother has completed all the requirements to make him _____ of being honored as an Eagle Scout.

7. Ted likes shopping for new _____ .

17

Letters	Examples	Sounds
sc	science	/s/
sc	scamper	/sk/
sc	conscious	/sh/

Directions: Circle each word in which the letters **sc** stand for /sk/. Underline each word in which **sc** stands for /s/. Draw a box around each word in which **sc** stands for /sh/.

1. In the television show Scarlet screamed and lost consciousness when she saw the scorpion.

2. The scorched scarf has the scent of smoke.

3. The actress scanned the script, then scoffed.

4. The scene I liked best in the movie showed the scientist discovering the mummy.

5. The famous restaurant has luscious scallops.

6. The sculptor constructed a scaffold around the marble before starting the work.

7. The scowl on the face of the movie monster did not scare the viewers.

8. Dave cut the seed packet with scissors, scooped up some seeds, then scattered a few into the hole he had dug.

9. The scarecrow discourages birds from scavenging the fields.

10. Stan was scared that the scratch would leave a scar.

11. Jesse squinted to see the score that was scrawled on the scoreboard.

12. Cindy was conscientious about learning her script for the class play.

● The letters **gn** in a word can stand for the sound /n/.

Directions: Read each sentence and notice the word in dark print. Then use the sentence to help you figure out the meaning of that word. Circle the letter of the correct meaning.

1. A swarm of small **gnats** flew in the warm summer air.

   a. tiny two-winged insects   b. old-fashioned fighter planes   c. spider-like animals

2. The car dealer just received a large **consignment** of brand-new cars.

   a. contract   b. parking lot   c. shipment

3. The cover of this book has a plaid **design.**

   a. lettering   b. pattern   c. signature

4. Tony knew that the newspaper was **foreign** because it was written in French.

   a. from the midwest   b. from another country   c. from Spain

5. That **cologne** smells like roses.

   a. paint   b. bonfire   c. perfume

6. The student **feigned** illness to get the teacher's sympathy.

   a. pretended   b. limped   c. got hurt

7. The **sovereign** governed the country with great wisdom and fairness.

   a. clown   b. ruler   c. traveler

Directions: Use a word in dark print from the exercise above to complete each of the following sentences.

1. Geoffrey's go-cart _____ won first prize in the contest.
2. When an enemy uncovered a nest containing the pheasant's young, the adult

   pheasant _____ injury to fool the enemy.

3. Our scout troop finally received our _____ of cookies to sell.

4. Stacy's _____ smells like lilacs.
5. Uncle Dan's car had the steering wheel on the right-hand side instead of the left,

   so we knew that the car was _____.
6. The small insects we saw when we were camping were either mosquitoes or

   _____.

7. Queen Elizabeth I was _____ of England when the ships of the Spanish Armada were defeated.

19

Letters	Examples	Sound
rh	rhyme	/r/
wr	wrist	/r/

Directions: Read the words below. Underline each word in which you see **rh.** Circle each word in which you see **wr.**

rhythm	wrench	wreath	unwrapped	wrinkle
wrens	rhinestones	wring	rhododendron	handwriting
rheumatism	awry	rhapsody	shipwrecked	wrong

Directions: Use a word from the list above to complete each sentence.

1. Dale saved the bread crumbs to feed them to the _____.

2. Rhonda's costume had glittering _____ on the skirt.

3. Meg's _____ used to be sloppy, but it has improved this year and we can read it.

4. The plumber used a _____ to tighten the pipes.

5. Grandma's _____ bush is growing below her kitchen window.

6. Sandy's scarf was so wet she had to _____ it out.

7. Jeff was surprised when he _____ his birthday gift.

8. Matthew carefully ironed his shirt to get rid of every _____ .

9. The whole class clapped to the _____ of the music.
10. *The Swiss Family Robinson* is about a family who lives on an island after they are

_____ .

20

Letters	Examples	Sounds
ear	clear	/ear/
ear	pear	/air/
ear	pearl	/ur/

Directions: Read each sentence and underline each **ear** word. Then write each word you underlined in the correct list below.

1. Earl earned enough money to go to camp.

2. Sailors can get their bearings by looking at the North Star.

3. It was clear that Bertha didn't want to wear her raincoat.

4. The pear tree is near the rear door.

5. We searched the woods for bear tracks.

6. I fear that Beth's earrings are lost.

7. Ted's new shirt had a large tear and was smeared with grease.

8. Ernest heard the song of the whippoorwills before the sun appeared.

9. Early humans often used a spear for hunting.

10. The tilt of the earth's axis causes the yearly change of seasons.

ear as in pear

_____   _____   _____

_____   _____

ear as in pearls

_____   _____   _____

_____   _____   _____

ear as in ear

_____   _____   _____

_____   _____   _____

_____   _____   _____

Directions: Work the crossword puzzle by thinking of a word containing **ear** to fit each definition.

Across

2. to gain knowledge
5. hair on the face
6. eager and serious
8. a wheel that has teeth that fit into another wheel
10. listen to
11. ornaments for the ears

Down

1. afraid of nothing
3. close
4. an animal that is one year old
6. wages or money paid to a person
7. a name for someone who is much loved
9. tired

Letters	Examples	Sound
are	care	/air/
air	hair	/air/

Directions: Read the words below. Underline each word in which you see **are**. Circle each word in which you see **air**.

shared	pair	scared	dairy	lair
square	repaired	aircraft	pares	fair
bare	stared	careful	fares	stairs

Directions: Use a word from the list above to complete each sentence.

1. A _____ is a figure drawn using four straight lines of equal length.

2. Carlos felt _____ when he heard a strange sound coming from the dark building.

3. Bob _____ his bicycle tire before he rode to the park.

4. Clair usually _____ apples before she eats them.

5. Diane bought a new _____ of running shoes.

6. Blair is always _____ to measure exactly when he cooks.

7. Milk, cheese, and ice cream are _____ products.

8. In the summer I like to walk in _____ feet.

9. Lisa, Ann, and Larry _____ the pizza equally.

10. Helicopters and jets are two kinds of _____ .

11. Mary thought that the umpire made a _____ decision.

12. We all _____ at Jim's weird Halloween costume.

13. Aunt Jan paid our taxi _____ .

14. Running up and down _____ is good exercise.

15. A _____ is the den or resting place of a wild animal.

Directions: Complete the unfinished word in each sentence by filling in the letters **ild** or **ind.**

1. Did you rem_____ Patty to bring her permission slip?

2. My grandpa likes to tell us about his ch_____hood.

3. My little sister just learned to sing "Three Bl_____ Mice."

4. Did you f_____ the sweater that you lost?

5. The recipe calls for two teaspoons of grated orange r_____.

6. The valley was filled with gorgeous blue w_____ flowers.

7. Grandma's k_____ness shows in all her actions.

Directions: Complete the unfinished word in each sentence by filling in the letters **ost** or **old.**

1. Gerry has a m_____ for making candles.

2. As the moviegoers watched and listened, a gh_____ly wail pierced the silence.

3. Nancy enjoys h_____ing her new baby brother.

4. Today was a c_____ day, but we played outside during recess anyway.

5. The p_____mark on the letter showed that it had been mailed from Toronto.

6. Rebecca won first prize in our school's safety p_____er contest.

7. The football sailed over the crossbar of our goal p_____, and the field goal was good.

● A word has as many syllables as it has vowel sounds.

Directions: Read the rule above. Then write the words having one syllable in column 1, those with two syllables in column 2, and those with three syllables in column 3.

disappear	dare	grind	numb	wheat
bold	climber	wholesome	whose	find
unique	questionnaire	meanwhile	cashier	declare
innermost	honeycomb	refreshment	overwhelm	chandelier
		foremost		

1
One Syllable

_____

_____

_____

_____

_____

_____

_____

2
Two Syllables

_____

_____

_____

_____

_____

_____

_____

3
Three Syllables

_____

_____

_____

_____

_____

_____

_____

Directions: Read the rules. Then divide the words into syllables by drawing vertical lines.

● When a single consonant comes between two vowels in a word, the word is usually divided after the consonant if the first vowel is short.

mod/el   rob/in

● When a single consonant comes between two vowels in a word, the word is usually divided before the consonant if the first vowel is long.

na/ture   ba/con

melon _____	final _____
facial _____	recent _____
silent _____	bison _____
lemon _____	finish _____
comic _____	magic _____
repair _____	rotate _____
cabin _____	petal _____
benign _____	pilot _____
declare _____	punish _____
visit _____	medal _____
pities _____	cities _____
modest _____	radish _____
design _____	famous _____
nasal _____	patient _____
music _____	lizard _____

Directions: Read the list of words. Then read through the story. Write the correct word from the list on the line to complete each unfinished sentence. Each list word contains a sound that you have already studied.

they	fearful	grind	holds
through	most	methods	beneath
humankind	scientific	earth	ancient

Earthquakes have happened many times _____ the ages. People
                                                    1

have been both _____ and curious when they unexpectedly felt the
                        2

usually solid earth suddenly tremble and quake _____ their feet.
                                                        3

_____ has always tried to explain and predict this mysterious and
        4

terrifying occurrence. For example, the ancient Greeks explained earthquakes by saying

that _____ happened because the sea god Poseidon was shattering rocks
        5

and shaking the land every time he was angry at a giant named Polybotes.

When scientists first began studying earthquakes, it almost seemed that the

_____ Greeks were right. Scientists found that _____
        6   7

earthquakes *do* happen beneath the ocean. But the cause of earthquakes is not gods
battling giants.

Today, scientific _____ of earthquake study have brought us new
                        8

knowledge. We know that earthquakes are caused by unstable sections of rock that shift

and _____ against each other under the earth's surface.
        9

The study of earthquakes has helped scientists find out much about the interior of the

_____. But there is much more to learn. Secrets the earth still holds
        10

include both the timing of future earthquakes and methods for gauging their severity.

Directions: Now use the list words to answer the questions below.

1. Which words contain the same **th** sound as the word *thin?*_____,

_____, _____, and _____.

2. Which word contains the same sound of *ear* heard in the word *clear?*

_____

3. Which word rhymes with *behind?* _____

Directions: Suppose that you are a volunteer in a place that has been hit by an earthquake. A reporter is asking you about the earthquake and about your role in helping the victims. Use the words in the list to answer the reporter's questions. Be sure to answer each question with a complete sentence so that you will be clearly understood.

health	overwrought	fearful	weary	kindness	find
search	mother	father	brother	sympathy	careful

Reporter: What was it like when the earthquake hit?

You: _____

_____

Reporter: How have the volunteers helped the victims of this crisis?

You: _____

_____

Reporter: What belongings were lost during the quake, and how will the owners go about recovering them?

You: _____

_____

Reporter: Have most of the family members involved been reunited?

You: _____

_____

Proofread your sentences.
Does each sentence begin with a capital letter and end with the correct punctuation? _____

Does each sentence make sense? _____

● The vowel digraph **ai** can stand for the long sound of **a** that you hear in the word **aim.**

Directions: Read each sentence. Draw a line under each word that contains the long sound of **a.** Then circle the letters that stand for that sound.

1. I went to the post office to mail the package to Canada.

2. It took three painters almost a whole week to finish painting our school.

3. We waited in vain for over an hour, but the train never passed us.

4. "Hurry!" Harry exclaimed. "We don't want to get caught in the rain!"

5. I asked if more of these dainty little pails were available.

6. When the power failure left us without electricity, we entertained ourselves by sitting by the fire and telling stories.

7. I explained that I planned to wear my new shirt to the party.

8. Pat remained after the party to help Scott clean up the stains in the carpet.

● The vowel digraph **ay** also can stand for the long sound of **a.**

Directions: Draw a line under the word in each row that contains the long sound of **a.** Then circle the letters that stand for that sound.

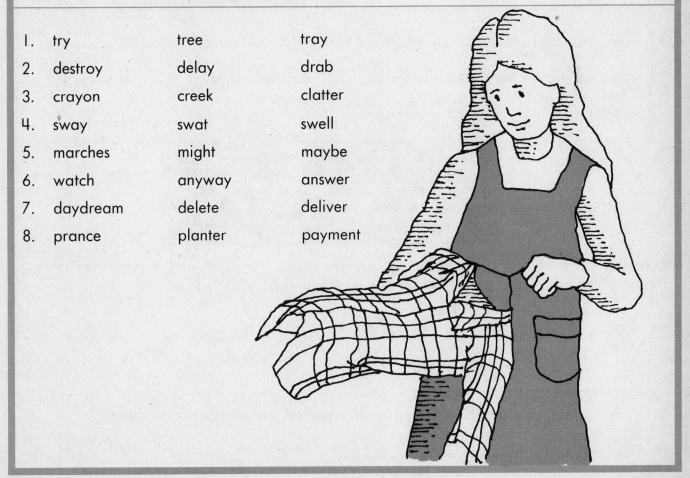

1.	try	tree	tray
2.	destroy	delay	drab
3.	crayon	creek	clatter
4.	sway	swat	swell
5.	marches	might	maybe
6.	watch	anyway	answer
7.	daydream	delete	deliver
8.	prance	planter	payment

29

Directions: Correctly complete each incomplete word in the sentences by adding the letters **ai** or **ay.**

1. Linda's mother took us out on the lake in her s_____lboat.

2. The pl_____ground does not open until nine o'clock.

3. Martha said that she would be aw_____ on vacation all next week.

4. We were able to tr_____n our pets to do several tricks.

5. "It has r_____ned every d_____ this week," Jonathan compl_____ned.

6. We hoped that no one would betr_____ our plans for Barry's surprise party.

7. This cereal contains several different gr_____ns and also has lots of r_____sins in it.

8. My spr_____ned ankle was p_____nful, but it didn't ruin my holid_____.

9. It did not take long for that str_____ cat to become a f_____thful member of our family.

10. I was afr_____d that gr_____ walls would make the room seem too pl_____n.

11. Julie waved back g_____ly when she had gotten midw_____ up the tr_____l.

12. Because of the storm, we had to del_____ our trip and rem_____n at home for a few more hours.

Directions: Use the words in the box to answer each of the questions below. Then circle the letters in each word that stand for the long sound of **a.**

gray day	pay day

1. What would you call a cloudy morning?

_____

2. What would you call the day you receive money you earned for working?

_____

● The vowel digraphs **ee** and **ei** can stand for the long sound of **e** that you hear in the words **see** and **seize.**

Directions: Circle the letters that stand for the long sound of **e** in each word. Then write each word in the correct column below.

needle	deceitful	receipt	Sheila
conceited	wheelbarrow	keeper	receiver
agreement	ceiling	steeple	greenhouse
beetle	succeed	protein	sleepy

see   **seize**

_____   _____

_____   _____

_____   _____

_____   _____

_____   _____

_____   _____

_____   _____

_____

Directions: Now use a word from the list on page 31 to complete each sentence.

1. _____ and Frank won the first prize in this year's science fair.

2. My uncle's hobby is gardening, and he keeps plants in his

   _____ all year long.

3. When we stopped at the bear's cage, a _____ reminded us that feeding the animals was against the rules.

4. The label on the package declared that this bread is rich in vitamins and

   _____.

5. Mr. Garcia gave us a _____ for the money that we deposited in the bank.

6. I rushed to answer the telephone, but it had stopped ringing by the time I picked up

   the _____.

7. Manny borrowed a _____ and some thread so he could mend the tear in his shirt.

8. Katherine's piano teacher told her that in order to _____ she has to work hard and practice often.

9. I know someone who is so _____ that he says he never makes mistakes.

10. Nicholas and Lee finally reached an _____ to divide the household chores evenly.

11. Joann is so _____ she can barely keep her eyes open.

12. Do you think it is _____ to promise to do something and then not keep your promise?

DO NOT FEED

● The vowel digraphs **oa, oe,** and **ow** can stand for the long sound of **o.**

Directions: Read each sentence. Draw a line under each word that has the long sound of **o.** Then circle the letters that stand for that sound.

1. Sandy and I tried to coax the goat from the barn.
2. Betty tiptoed because she did not want to wake her sister.
3. I tried to throw the softball the farthest.
4. Snowflakes fell and piled up on the roadway.
5. I stubbed my toe as I climbed from the boat.
6. It did not take me long to outgrow that coat.
7. The stowaway on Mika's sailboat was her collie, Charlie.
8. I fixed myself a bowl of hot oatmeal for breakfast.
9. Clark boasted that he was the faster runner, and he wanted to show me.
10. Tim used the hoe to pull the weeds from each row of vegetables in the garden.

Directions: Complete the unfinished word in each sentence by writing letters **oa, oe,** or **ow** on the line.

1. Yesterday afternoon we baked three l_____ves of bread.

2. My pencil broke, and I had to borr_____ one from my friend.

3. I had a p_____ched egg and some t_____st for breakfast.

4. Dana had a w_____ful look on her face when she learned that the tennis match had been cancelled.

5. The water in the river is too shall_____ for your b_____t.

6. I had never fl_____n in an airplane until we took our trip to Toronto last year.

7. My voice was hoarse from cheering, and the only sound that came from my

   thr_____t was a quiet gr_____n.

8. Have you ever noticed your shad_____ walking ahead of you along the r_____d?

9. Patricia's claim that she could make a rainb_____ in her backyard was no

   h_____x!

10. Stan never gl_____ts about it, but he is the best b_____ler on our team.

Directions: Nineteen words in which the vowel digraphs **oa, oe,** and **ow** have the long sound of **o** are hidden in the puzzle below. Some go across, and others go up and down. Circle each word as you find it in the puzzle, then write the word under the correct heading.

```
S  C  A  R  E  C  R  O  W  L  A  I  S  O  W
H  F  M  A  N  X  F  O  E  C  L  O  A  D  I
O  I  T  T  H  R  O  W  T  D  O  E  Z  Y  S
W  R  O  O  S  T  P  E  L  M  M  O  A  N  G
B  C  S  R  Y  B  E  F  O  B  L  R  E  N  T
T  E  L  O  D  E  T  O  A  D  S  T  O  O  L
O  T  O  W  C  C  A  A  Y  F  A  N  T  Y  E
M  M  A  T  O  E  L  N  A  O  B  F  L  O  O
O  R  N  A  C  U  T  A  N  A  T  I  N  R  A
R  D  R  O  O  X  R  B  T  M  S  O  A  K  K
R  F  E  B  A  A  T  H  E  L  T  O  O  M  B
O  T  L  C  B  R  T  O  A  C  D  B  T  K  L
W  M  O  P  C  L  P  E  E  F  H  J  N  O  R
```

oa	oe	ow

_____ _____ _____

_____ _____ _____

_____ _____ _____

_____   _____

_____   _____

_____

Directions: Use a word that you found in the puzzle to complete each sentence below.

1. After ice skating in the cold, we drank hot _____ to help warm us.

2. _____ we will row the boat on the lake.

Directions: Read the article below. Complete each finished word by writing one of the vowel digraphs **ai, ay, ee, ei, oa, oe,** or **ow** on the line.

Life was not easy for the people who came to the coast of North America in colonial

d_____s. But they were determined to st_____ here, and they worked hard to
     1   2

succ_____d. One of the m_____n occupations was farming. Many colonial families each
      3   4

m_____nt_____ned their _____n small farms where they r_____sed livestock, gr_____n,
    5   6   7   8   9

and other crops. The rocky terr_____n and harsh weather made it difficult for the farmers
                              10

to gr_____ more than what they needed to f_____d themselves.
      11   12

In other parts of New England, people earned their livings in different w_____s.
                                                                         13

Along the coast, fishing was important to many colonists. B_____t building was also
                                                            14

important to the c_____stal area, and many people cl_____med that ships built there
                  15   16

were the best afl_____t. Lumber for these ships came from nearby forests of _____ks
                   17   18

and evergr_____ns.
          19

Other colonists worked as storek_____pers and merchants. They bought local
                                 20

products and sent them to Europe. The money they rec_____ved for these goods was
                                                  21

used as p_____ment for things they knew their fellow colonists would buy—such as sugar,
         22

molasses, clothes, hammers, n_____ls, and h_____s. As the merchants became more
                            23   24

successful, the small towns grew, and soon the colonial areas b_____sted several
                                                              25

important cities.

Good writers never just "write something." They give themselves a second chance by revising what they wrote. They look over what they have written to check for things that may not be correct, and they try to improve what they have written.

What do good writers look for when they go to revise their work? One of the first things they do is check to see that each paragraph contains one topic or idea.

Directions: Read the paragraph below and find the sentence that does not belong in the paragraph.

One of the main occupations in colonial North America was farming. Many colonial families lived and worked on their own small farms. The soil was rocky, and the weather was harsh. Fishing and shipbuilding provided jobs for those who lived along the Atlantic coast. The farmers usually could grow only enough to feed themselves.

You probably noticed that four of the five sentences in the paragraph are about farming in colonial North America. The fourth sentence, however, is about fishing and shipbuilding. It does not belong in this paragraph.

Directions: Now read the paragraph below. Find the sentences that do not belong in this paragraph. Then rewrite the paragraph, leaving out the sentences that do not belong.

Boat building was also important, and many colonists worked building ships. North American merchants shipped local products to England. When their ships returned, they carried the goods needed by the colonists. Fishing was one of the most important occupations in coastal towns. The lively trade kept up by these merchants helped keep the colonies supplied with sugar, clothing, and tools. The merchants and storekeepers were important to the growth of the small towns into cities.

_____

_____

_____

_____

_____

_____

_____

_____

_____

Directions: Read each sentence below. Draw a line under each word that contains the long sound of **a.** Then circle the letters that stand for that sound.

1.   Liz held tightly to the reins as her horse galloped onto the field.

2.   The picture of my mother's grandmother shows her wearing a hat with a veil.

3.   Reindeer are found in the wild in some countries of northern Europe.

4.   The Revolutionary War occurred during the reign of King George III of England.

5.   A rich vein of gold ore was found in the mine.

Directions: Read each word listed below. Circle the letters that stand for the long sound of **a.** Then write the number of the word on the line in front of its definition.

1.   convey   _____   to do what one is told or asked

2.   obey   _____   to look over carefully

3.   prey   _____   to take from one place to another

4.   survey   _____   a creature that is hunted or seized by another

Directions: Look back at the letters you circled, and complete the rule below.

The vowel digraphs _____ and _____ can stand for the long sound of **a.**

37

● The vowel digraph **ea** can stand for the long sound of **a** that you hear in the word **break** or the short sound of **e** that you hear in the word **head**. Ea also can stand for the regular double vowel sound of long **e** that you hear in the word **leaf**.

Directions: Read each sentence. Draw a line under the word in each sentence that contains the double vowel **ea**. Then circle the sound that **ea** stands for in that word.

1. We planned to go on our camping trip at daybreak. /ā/ /ĕ/ /ē/

2. My sister reminded me not to ski bareheaded in the cold wind. /ā/ /ĕ/ /ē/

3. The Hill School Lions defeated our tennis players at the big match. /ā/ /ĕ/ /ē/

4. Charlene's new sweater is gray and blue. /ā/ /ĕ/ /ē/

5. The scientists hope that the new medicine will prevent an outbreak of flu. /ā/ /ĕ/ /ē/

6. My arms were sore after I helped knead the clay. /ā/ /ĕ/ /ē/

7. I told Mary about the pheasant that I saw running across our yard into the bushes. /ā/ /ĕ/ /ē/

8. Martin is one of the kindest, most easygoing people that I know. /ā/ /ĕ/ /ē/

9. I usually have eggs and toast for breakfast. /ā/ /ĕ/ /ē/

10. I finally found my bathing suit underneath my record collection. /ā/ /ĕ/ /ē/

11. The roof of our treehouse is leaky, and we will have to fix it. /ā/ /ĕ/ /ē/

12. This morning, we rowed all the way out to the breakwater and went fishing. /ā/ /ĕ/ /ē/

13. I thought for weeks until I finally thought of a place to conceal my brother's birthday present. /ā/ /ĕ/ /ē/

14. We will always treasure our memories of this trip to the lake. /ā/ /ĕ/ /ē/

15. They measured the inside of the tent to make sure that all the belongings would fit inside. /ā/ /ĕ/ /ē/

Directions: Read each sentence. Find the two words with the double vowel **ea** and draw a line under them. Then circle the double vowel in each one. Then write each word you underlined in the correct column below.

1. "That was a great steak!" Bonnie exclaimed as she finished her dinner.

2. Daniel spread homemade jam on a slice of fresh bread.

3. I walked to the end of the diving board and held myself steady until I was ready to jump.

4. It is always a pleasure to have such lovely weather as this.

5. My father said that he would teach me how to bleach clothes.

6. "It's quite a feat," said Sam, "to keep your room so neat."

ea sounded as /ā/	**ea** sounded as /ĕ/	**ea** sounded as /ē/
_____	_____	_____
_____	_____	_____
	_____	_____
	_____	_____
	_____	
	_____	

● The vowel digraphs **au** and **aw** stand for the same sound. They stand for the vowel sound you hear in **draw** and **August.**

Directions: Complete each unfinished word in the sentences by filling in the letters **au** or **aw.**

1. Claude had to withdr_____ some money from his piggy bank to buy a birthday present for his grandma.

2. Mary helped fix the leaky f_____cet.

3. I stacked my socks neatly in the dresser dr_____er.

4. We scattered str_____ over the freshly seeded l_____n.

5. I asked the _____thor of the book if he would write his _____tograph inside the front cover for me.

6. Chris and Joan were exh_____sted after jogging six miles this morning.

7. A fl_____ in the glass bowl c_____sed it to break when Claudia set it down.

8. Every _____tumn my family takes an _____tomobile drive to see the brightly colored leaves.

9. Kay and Lee watched the g_____ky little f_____n take its first steps.

10. I was so tired that I had to work _____fully hard to keep from y_____ning during the band concert.

Directions: Write the number of each word on the line beside its meaning.

1. **shawl** _____ a small, shallow dish to put a cup on

2. **cautious** _____ to unfreeze

3. **applaud** _____ not graceful; clumsy

4. **thaw** _____ to express approval by clapping the hands

5. **awkward** _____ a large pot or kettle

6. **saucer** _____ bite, chew, or wear away

7. **gnaw** _____ a piece of cloth worn around a person's shoulders

8. **cauldron** _____ very careful

40

Directions: Use the words in the list to find the name for each picture. Then write the word that names each picture on the line below it.

wiener	tie	shield
pie	thief	field

_____   _____   _____

_____   _____   _____

Directions: Say the words in the list above. Circle the letters that stand for the vowel sound in each word. Look at the letters that you just circled. Now use the words to help complete the rule below.

The vowel digraph **ie** can stand for the long sound of _____ that you hear in the words

_____, _____, _____, and _____. It can also stand for the long sound of

_____ that you hear in the words _____ and _____.

41

Directions: Complete each sentence by unscrambling the letters under the line to make a word.

1. I _____ for over a week, but I was
   deirt
   not able to teach my gerbil to fetch the newspaper.

2. Meg and Tim _____ for joy when
   reishked
   they learned that they had won the trip to the zoo.

3. Our math homework for tonight is _____
   fierb
   enough for me to finish in an hour.

4. Because Mr. Thomas was so _____ with the job I had done cutting
   tisadeifs
   his lawn, he asked if I could cut the grass every week.

5. The _____ of our car is so dirty that it is hard to see through it.
   weidnidshl

Directions: In each sentence below, circle any word in which the vowel digraph **ie** stands for the long sound of **i**. Draw one line under any word in which the digraph **ie** stands for the long sound of **e**. Then write each word in the correct column.

1. For some reason, it took me a long time to finally learn how to tie and untie my shoelaces.
2. I stared at the coach in disbelief when she told me that I would get to play left field in tomorrow's game.
3. Mary gave a brief and very dignified reply to the rude question.
4. Danny believes that the chief reason why our team always lost was that we never tried hard enough.
5. Mark's sister Beth said that it was a relief to know that she had qualified for her driver's license.

ie sounded as /ī/

_____   _____

_____   _____   _____

ie sounded as /ē/

_____   _____   _____

_____   _____   _____

Directions: The words in the list have letters and sounds that you studied in this unit. Read the words. Then read the paragraphs below. Choose the correct word from the list to complete each unfinished sentence in the paragraphs. Use your dictionary if you need to.

heyday	saw	dissatisfied	tried
automatically	toiled	countries	already
factories	Northeast	brief	overseas
awful	stream	cause	thread
great	spread	they	least

People who lived in America during the first half of the 1800's _____ major

changes in their way of life. One _____ of these _____ changes was the use of machinery to make things that once had been made only by human hands.

Factories first appeared in the _____ in New England. For a long time, New England had been a center of the textile, or cloth-making, industry. At first, cloth and

_____ had been made by hand by people who worked in their own homes. But soon, spinning and weaving machines were developed that could make these products

almost _____ . With these machines, a person could produce at _____ ten times as much cloth as before.

The first American textile plant was built in Pawtucket, Rhode Island, near a river that

provided water power for the machines. Soon, _____ and machines _____ across the country until it seemed that there was a factory beside every river and

_____! The _____ of machines had begun, and in a few, _____ years, much of the countryside changed completely.

Where did the workers for these factories come from? Some were in New England

_____ working on small, poor farms. Many of these farmers _____ factory

work. Other workers came from foreign _____. These people came to North

America from _____ to work in the factories.

Life in the factories could be _____ at times. Men, women, and children might work 18 hours a day, 6 days a week. Many times they were paid less than $2 a week.

For these people, factory life was hard, and many were _____ enough to leave.

Others decided that factory life was not worse than what _____ had had before, and they stayed.

● **Sequence** is the order in which things happen. It's important to check that you have put details in the proper sequence.

Directions: In the paragraph below things are not described in the correct sequence. Read the paragraph and figure out what is wrong.

The factories that came to New England completely changed this. With the factories came spinning and weaving machines. When people used machines instead of their hands, they could produce ten times as much cloth as before. Until the 1800's, people made cloth and thread by hand, working in their own homes.

You probably noticed that the details in the paragraph do not make much sense because a sentence is out of sequence.

Directions: Read the paragraph again. Write the sentences in the correct order on the lines below.

_____

_____

_____

_____

_____

_____

_____

_____

_____

● One of the sounds the vowel digraph **oo** stands for is the vowel sound you hear in **too** and **moon**. Another sound that **oo** can stand for is the vowel sound you hear in **look** and **good**.

Directions: Write the correct name for each picture. Then circle the letters that stand for the vowel sound that you hear in that name.

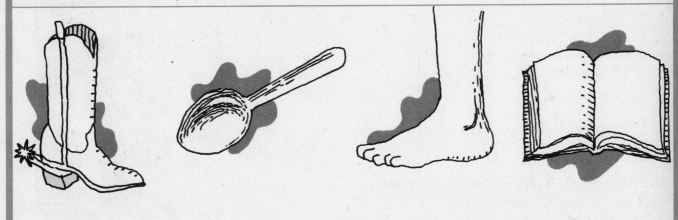

_____   _____   _____   _____

Directions: Read the poem. Circle each word that contains the vowel digraph **oo**. Then write each word you circled in the correct column. Use each word only once.

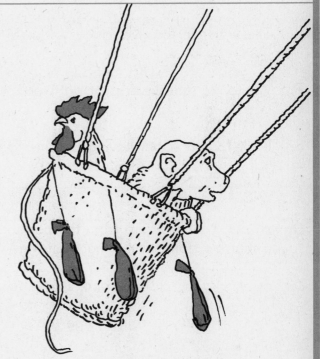

Nosey the snoopy rooster

And Ray the laughing baboon

Took off on a flight

Last Monday night

In Ray's wooden balloon.

Right through a typhoon

They sailed until noon,

But soon they came down with a swoop.

"Look, you can't fly all day,"

Said Nosey to Ray,

"When you've got termites

In your balloon!"

oo as in boot   **oo as in book**

_____   _____   _____

_____   _____   _____

_____   _____   _____

45

● The vowel digraph **oo** can also stand for the vowel sound that you hear in **flood.** Here are three sounds that the vowel **oo** can stand for: /o͞o/ as in **moon;** /o͝o/ as in **look;** /ŭ/ as in **flood.**

Directions: Read each sentence. Draw a line under the word in the sentence that contains the vowel digraph **oo.** Then circle the sound that the digraph **oo** stands for in that word.

1. Each of us brought something to our classroom picnic.

   /o͞o/ /o͝o/ /ŭ/

2. Bob and Sondra showed me their pet bloodhound.

   /o͞o/ /o͝o/ /ŭ/

3. Giving our dog a shampoo was not an easy job.

   /o͞o/ /o͝o/ /ŭ/

4. We ran outside and made footprints in the freshly fallen snow.

   /o͞o/ /o͝o/ /ŭ/

5. Nicholas loaned me some paper from his notebook.

   /o͞o/ /o͝o/ /ŭ/

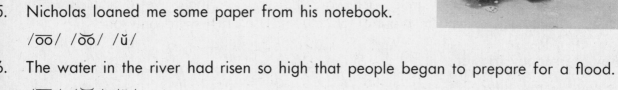

6. The water in the river had risen so high that people began to prepare for a flood.

   /o͞o/ /o͝o/ /ŭ/

7. We found many pieces of driftwood as we walked along the shore.

   /o͞o/ /o͝o/ /ŭ/

8. I felt foolish about having become so upset about something as silly as a game.

   /o͞o/ /o͝o/ /ŭ/

Directions: Use a phrase from the box to answer each question below. Then circle the sound that **oo** stands for in each answer.

shook book	tooth booth	hoop troop

1. What would you call a large group of basketball players?

   _____   /o͞o/ /o͝o/ /ŭ/

2. What would you call a place where you could go to buy new teeth whenever you wanted them?

   _____   /o͞o/ /o͝o/ /ŭ/

3. What would you call a dictionary that fell from the library's top shelf?

   _____   /o͞o/ /o͝o/ /ŭ/

Directions: Read each sentence below. Then circle the letters that stand for the vowel sound you hear in each word in dark print.

1. Martha and Brian **built** a new house for their dog, Sam.

2. I had a piece of fresh **fruit** for dessert.

3. My great-grandma made the **quilt** on my bed over fifty years ago.

4. This year, Aunt Catherine and Uncle Chuck are going on a **cruise** during their vacation.

Directions: Now complete the rule below. The sounds that stand for the letters that you circled will help you.

- The vowel digraph **ui** can _____ the sound of **i** that you hear in **built** or the long sound of **oo** that you hear in **fruit.**

Directions: Complete each sentence below by unscrambling the letters to make a word.

1. I started taking _____ lessons last month, and already I can play
   utagri

   twelve chords.

2. Mother took her new _____ to a tailor to have some alterations
   tius

   made.

3. My sister Renee asked that I not stay around making a _____ of
   cisanune

   myself when her friends are visiting her.

4. Denny and I fixed homemade _____ and ate them for breakfast this
   tisubics

   morning.

5. I felt _____ about forgetting
   lutygi

   to send my uncle a birthday card.

47

Directions: Draw a line under the word in each sentence that contains the vowel digraph **ui.** Then write the word in the correct column below.

1. The apple that I ate this afternoon with lunch was juicy and delicious.

2. My doctor's office is in the gray building on the corner of Water and North Clark streets.

3. I bruised my knee when I fell off my skateboard, but the fall wasn't too painful.

4. Marge said that she didn't think that orange, green, and pink made a suitable combination for our new school colors.

5. When Ben caught the ball and ran, the rest of us took off in pursuit.

6. The city announced that there were plans to rebuild the houses that had been destroyed in the earthquake.

7. The police officer showed the students the new cruisers that the department had ordered.

ui sounded as /i/   **ui** sounded as /o͞o/

_____   _____   _____

_____   _____

                    _____

                    _____

Directions: Read the words in the list. Then read the paragraphs below. Write the word from the list that correctly completes each unfinished sentence.

build	foolish	soon	goods
floods	fruits	took	built

Have you ever seen a canal? A canal is a channel filled with water through which large ships can travel. During the early 1800's, canals were very important to people. Canals linked together many American cities, making it possible for boats to carry farm

products and manufactured _____ back and forth across the land.

The Erie Canal was one of the earliest and most important of such waterways to be

_____ . It joined the Hudson River in eastern New York State with the city of Buffalo on Lake Erie. This canal helped link New York City and the Great Lakes.

Work on the Erie Canal began in 1817. Thousands of workers were needed for the job of digging the "big ditch," as it was called. The laborers endured sickness, hunger,

and even _____ . It _____ eight years and seven million dollars to

_____ the canal. When it was finished in 1825, there was a channel 363 miles (594 km) long and 4 feet deep. It was wide enough for several boats to pass at the same time.

How successful was the canal? Had it been _____ to spend so much time, money, and effort on a big ditch? When the canal was finished, the cost of shipping goods between New York City and Buffalo fell from $100 to just $10 per ton. Over

13,000 trips were made through the canal in its first year alone. _____ , farm

products of all kinds—meat, grain, _____ , vegetables—were traveling eastward and westward faster than before.

49

Revising what you have written gives you a chance to make your writing more interesting and easier to read. When you look over what you have written, ask yourself these questions:

● Do the words I have used *help* the reader understand what I am trying to say?

● Have I given interesting details that help the reader *see* what is being described?

● Have I used colorful words that will make what I have written seem *interesting* and *exciting* to the reader?

Directions: Read each pair of sentences below. Circle the numeral of the sentence that gives a better picture.

1. Many workers were needed for the job of digging the canal.

2. Thousands of workers were needed for the job of digging this "big ditch" across New York State.

1. When finished, the canal was long and wide and a few feet deep.

2. The Erie Canal measured 363 miles long and four feet deep when it was finished in 1825.

Did you notice that in both examples, the second sentence contains more details to help the reader form a better picture of what is being described?

Directions: Revise the paragraph below. Use details from the article on page 49 to make the paragraph more interesting.

It took several years and much money to build the canal. The people who did the work endured many hardships. But the canal was worth the effort. It cost less money to ship goods. Many trips were made through the canal.

_____

_____

_____

_____

_____

_____

_____

● A diphthong is made up of two vowels sounded so that the sound of both vowels can be heard blended together as one sound. The diphthongs **oi** and **oy** stand for the same sound. They stand for the vowel sound you hear in **oil** and **toy.**

Directions: Under each picture write the word that goes with it. Then circle the letters that stand for the vowel sound in that word.

royalty   cowboy   noisemakers   coin   boy   soil

_____   _____   _____   _____

Directions: Write the diphthong **oi** or **oy** to correctly complete the unfinished word in each sentence.

1. The soil in the garden was still m_____st from last night's rain.

2. Tamara said that she was sure we would enj_____ the circus.

3. Jack was wearing his favorite cordur_____ suit.

4. Mom and Dad are always careful to lock up any chemicals that might be harmful or

   p_____sonous.

5. Marcia asked us not to ann_____ her pets in the hot weather.

Directions: In the puzzle there are words containing the diphthongs **oi** and **oy.** Circle each of those words in the puzzle. Then write them on the lines at the right.

L	M	I	O	S	Y	O	T
O	L	T	P	O	I	N	T
Y	T	A	M	I	Y	M	S
A	E	N	B	L	U	R	P
L	T	O	I	L	R	E	O
A	J	I	L	M	O	D	I
W	O	S	O	I	Y	E	L
R	I	Y	O	U	A	N	E
A	N	A	B	I	L	T	D

_____

_____

_____

_____

_____

_____

_____

_____

Directions: The definition for each word in the first column can be found in the second column. Write the letter of each definition on the line next to the word that goes with it. Circle the diphthong in each word.

_____ 1. recoil

_____ 2. convoy

_____ 3. turmoil

_____ 4. employer

_____ 5. disappoint

_____ 6. destroy

_____ 7. avoid

_____ 8. voyage

A. a person who provides jobs for others

B. to ruin; put an end to; break in pieces

C. to fail to satisfy someone's wishes

D. to keep away from; not see or use

E. to draw or shrink back in dislike or fear

F. a group of vehicles gathered together for protection

G. a journey or trip, usually by sea

H. noise; disturbance; commotion

Directions: Now use one of the words from above to complete each of the following sentences.

1. My mom's _____ told her she will receive a promotion.

2. There was so much _____ during the clearance sale at the department store, that I never saw the friend I was supposed to meet.

3. The citizens want to make sure that the new dam will not _____ the forests they enjoy.

4. When the first snowstorm struck, the trucks formed a _____ to make their way over the slippery roads.

5. Grandma will bring the photos that she took during her _____ across the ocean.

6. I usually try to _____ eating foods that I think are fattening.

7. The sight of the garden snake startled me and made me _____ in surprise.

8. Mary hopes she will not _____ me, but she will not be able to go to summer camp this year.

● The diphthong **ew** stands for the vowel sound you hear in **new.** This is nearly the same vowel sound you hear in **spoon.**

Directions: Circle the diphthong in each of the words in the list.

newspaper	shrewd	pewter	jeweler
nephew	renewal	steward	mildew

Directions: Complete each sentence with a word from the list above.

1. At the museum we saw some _____ mugs and plates that had been used by early colonists.

2. I read about last night's football game in this morning's _____.

3. It seems strange to me, but I have a niece and a _____ who are older than I am.

4. Marilyn says that she wants to work as a _____ after studying about minerals and gems.

5. Before we went camping this summer, we scrubbed the _____ from the roof of the tent.

Directions: Use a phrase from the list below to answer each question. Then circle the letters that make the vowel sound in each word.

few flew   stew crew   new dew

1. What would you call the fresh drops of water on the lawn each morning?

   _____

2. What would you say if only a couple of people took airplane trips today?

   _____

3. What would you call the twelve cooks who worked to make a stew?

   _____

53

Directions: Read the words in each row. Draw a line under the words that contain the same vowel sound. Then circle the letters that stand for that sound.

1.	growl	grunt	ground
2.	droop	drowsy	doubtful
3.	outbreak	floodlight	flower
4.	funny	power	foundation
5.	counter	prowl	prune
6.	unstable	eyebrow	compound
7.	mountainous	cow	explode
8.	scramble	slouch	downstream
9.	township	mouthful	tawny
10.	outweigh	rowdy	rusting

Directions: Use the letters you circled to help you complete the rule below.

● The diphthongs _____ and _____ often stand for the vowel sound you hear in **loud** and **down.**

Directions: Use a phrase from the list below to answer each question. Then circle the letters that make the vowel sound in each word.

sound pound   sour power   now chow   fowl towel

1. What would you call a cloth to wipe off a chicken?

   _____

2. What would you call sixteen ounces of noise?

   _____

3. What would you call the most up-to-date food?

   _____

4. What slogan could you use to advertise lemons?

   _____

Directions: Correctly complete each sentence by unscrambling the letters of the word below the line.

1. For the costume party, I dressed as a circus _____.
    wlcon

2. Tim and I had clam _____ for lunch today.
    hocerdw

3. The _____ said that the show would begin in five minutes.
    nocunnera

4. For some reason I have felt sleepy and _____.
    sryowd

5. It has rained _____ the day and night.
    gotruhuhot

Directions: At the bottom of the page is a list of answers to the questions below. Read each question, find the answer, and write it on the line.

1. We caught a **trout** today when we were fishing.
    What is a **trout?** _____

2. I **glower** at my brother when he plays my records without asking.

    What does **glower** mean? _____

3. Last week Mel had a **bout** of the flu.

    What is **bout?** _____

4. The bride and groom will exchange their **vows** at noon.

    What are **vows?** _____

to stare at angrily	a kind of fish	promises or pledges	period of time to have something

Directions: Say each word. Write the number of vowels you see and the number of vowel sounds you hear.

	Vowels Seen	Vowel Sounds Heard		Vowels Seen	Vowel Sounds Heard
remainder	_____	_____	restaurant	_____	_____
proceed	_____	_____	lawbreaker	_____	_____
mountain	_____	_____	conveyance	_____	_____
loafer	_____	_____	passageway	_____	_____
woeful	_____	_____	loaded	_____	_____
abstain	_____	_____	lawnmower	_____	_____
retreat	_____	_____	greedily	_____	_____
vein	_____	_____	receivable	_____	_____
daybreak	_____	_____	autograph	_____	_____
laundry	_____	_____	maroon	_____	_____
sprawl	_____	_____	waterproof	_____	_____
occupied	_____	_____	bountiful	_____	_____
toadstool	_____	_____	power	_____	_____
countless	_____	_____	misunderstood	_____	_____
likelihood	_____	_____	woodpecker	_____	_____
fried	_____	_____	flaunt	_____	_____
loosen	_____	_____	circuit	_____	_____
tablespoon	_____	_____	wheelbarrow	_____	_____
relieved	_____	_____	guitar	_____	_____
yield	_____	_____	suitable	_____	_____
applied	_____	_____	billow	_____	_____

Directions: Read the article below. Complete each unfinished word by writing the diphthong **oi, oy, ew, ou,** or **ow** on the line.

Do you know the story of h_____ Christopher Columbus came to discover America

by "mistake"? Supposedly, Columbus was so sure that the world was r_____nd, not flat, that he thought he could reach the Far East by sailing westward. As we know, Columbus's

v_____age led him to islands in the Caribbean, not to the East Indies near Asia. But it

seems to have taken some time before Columbus believed that he and his cr_____ had

touched gr_____nd in a "n_____ world" and not on an island off the coast of Japan or China.

Columbus was not the only European explorer whose discoveries came by accident or

mistake. Explorers like John Cabot first came to America in search of a short r_____te to

all_____ ships from Britain to reach China and India. Others made their journeys with more unusual goals in mind. The Spanish explorer, Juan Ponce de León, for example, was

searching for the "f_____ntain of youth" when he came upon an unsp_____led coast north of Puerto Rico. He explored that coast in 1513, thinking that he had discovered a

large island. He named it Florida which in Spanish means "full of fl_____ers."

Francisco Coronado was another explorer who was disapp_____nted in what he

f_____nd in the new world. Coronado came to the American S_____thwest in 1540. He was looking for the Seven Cities of Cibola, a group of cities where riches were supposed to be so plentiful that the streets were paved with gold. For several years, Coronado's

l_____al band searched the m_____ntains and deserts with_____t success. Coronado

never did find Cibola's gold and j_____els. What his army did find was the Grand Canyon, one of the most beautiful wonders of the world.

Directions: Read the article below. In each paragraph find one sentence that does not belong and draw a line through it. Finally, copy your revised article on the lines.

George Vancouver was born in Norfolk, England, in 1758. The British government sent a naval force, led by Vancouver to the area. At age 13, Vancouver served with Captain Cook on that famous explorer's last two voyages.

Later, Vancouver joined the navy. His ship set sail in April of 1791. In 1793, Vancouver explored part of the American West Coast. He sailed by the Cape of Good Hope, in Africa, and Australia and New Zealand, making maps of these areas as he traveled. Vancouver dealt with the situation at Nootka Sound promptly.

Vancouver is remembered as a British explorer who made some of the first maps of the South Pacific. He also surveyed the Pacific Coast of North America. Vancouver sailed in all kinds of weather. The charts Vancouver made of these areas were among the first maps Europeans had of the South Pacific. They proved extremely valuable to sailors in later years.

_____

_____

_____

_____

_____

_____

_____

_____

_____

_____

Many words have special parts, or units of meaning, that help the reader to understand what the word means.

Directions: Circle the answer that best completes each sentence.

1. A root is the most basic word part. Other word parts can be added to a root. **Kind** is the root of **unkindly.** The root of **unlawful** is _____.

           un   law   ful

2. The root of **uncover** is _____.

           uncover   un   cover

3. The root of **replaced** is _____.

           re   placed   place

4. A root contains _____.

           a prefix and a suffix   more than one word part   one word part

5. A prefix is a word part added **in front of** a root. **Un** is the prefix of **unhappy.** The prefix of **retied** is _____.

           ed   re   tie

6. The prefix of **misleading** is _____.

           lead   leading   mis

7. A prefix _____ the meaning of a root.

           changes   doesn't change   stops

8. A suffix is a word part added **in back of** a root. **Er** is the suffix of **worker.** The suffix of **action** is _____.

           act   ion   a

9. The suffix of **contentment** is _____.

           ment   tent   content

10. The suffix of **rewrites** is _____.

            re   s   writes

11. A word part or unit of meaning, can have _____.

            no letters   one letter   no sounds

Directions: Circle the answer that best completes each sentence.

1. **In** is the prefix of **insight** and **include.** The root of **insight** is _____.

   in   sight   insight

2. The root of **include** is _____.

   in   clude   include

3. A root _____ be a word itself.

   can   cannot

4. A root _____ **always** a word itself.

   is   is not

5. The root of **import** is **port.** The word **import** has _____ word part(s) or unit(s) of meaning.

   1   2   3

6. The word **important** has _____ word part(s).

   1   2   3

7. The word **importantly** has _____ word parts.

   2   3   4

8. The word part **able** can be a suffix. The word **portable** has _____ word part(s) or unit(s) of meaning.

   1   2   3

9. The word **transport** has _____ word part(s).

   1   2

10. The word **transportable** has _____ word parts.

    3   4   5

● **Un, dis, ir, im,** and **in** are prefixes that usually mean **not.**

word	definition
unhappy	not happy
disapprove	not approve
irregular	not regular
inexpensive	not expensive
impractical	not practical

Directions: Underline the word in each sentence that has a prefix meaning **not.** Then circle the prefix in that word.

1. A magician makes rabbits disappear.

2. A zigzag line is irregular.

3. The team was unbeatable.

4. Our plans are indefinite.

5. The twins are unlike each other.

6. The broken vase is irreparable.

7. Blue and red are dissimilar colors.

8. Neighbors disapproved of the pet lion.

9. Being dishonest is a bad habit.

10. The word *ain't* is improper English.

11. Rain is infrequent in the desert.

12. Wild animals are untamed.

Directions: In each sentence below, there is a word which is missing the prefix **un, dis, ir,** or **in.** Write the prefix in the space provided.

1. Wandering hunters of the Stone Age were _____civilized.

2. The game wasn't fun because the leader was _____organized.

3. Some mushrooms are _____edible.

4. A stomachache is an _____comfortable feeling.

5. Blue jeans and sneakers are _____formal clothes.

6. Ted and Susie were good friends, even though they often _____agreed.

Directions: Choose a word from the list that correctly completes each unfinished sentence below.

discolored	unfavorable	incomplete
irresponsible	disagreed	invalid
unbreakable	irrecoverable	insecure
inconvenient	discontented	disconnected

1. Susan was not satisfied with her finished painting. Susan was

   _____.

2. None of the glasses was broken, even though they had been dropped on the

   sidewalk. The glasses were _____.

3. Some pages were missing from Pilar's spelling book. The spelling book was

   _____.

4. The severe storm cut off phone service for three hours to the Wilsons' home. Their

   phone was _____.

5. Sam couldn't play baseball until 7:30, but the game started at 7:00. The starting

   time was _____ for Sam.

6. Hugh thought the science fiction movie was wonderful. Harry didn't like it at all.

   Hugh and Harry _____.

7. Over the years, the photo album had become stained and yellowed. The album had

   become _____.

8. Jeffrey promised to be home at 3:00, but he decided to play ball and didn't arrive

   until 4:30. Jeffrey was _____.

9. Pam's library card expired three months ago.

   Her card is now _____.

10. Black clouds fill the sky and the wind is strong.

    The weather is _____
    for a picnic.

11. The puppy was afraid away from its mother

    and in its new home. The puppy felt _____.

● **In** and **en** are prefixes that can mean **cause to be** or **make.**

word	definition
indent	make a line begin farther in
entangle	to cause something to be tangled

Directions: Choose the word that best completes each sentence, and write it on the line.

1. The Inca Indians _____ South American culture.

                entitled   enriched   intoned

2. The map of the United States had an _____ that showed Hawaii and Alaska.

                inset   intake   ensnarl

3. The choir leader _____ the song and then all joined in.

                inflated   intoned   inhaled

4. Heavy coats and boots _____ that the hikers would be warm even in cold weather.

                enraptured   ensured   inscribed

5. The workers will _____ the street so that more traffic can drive through the area.

                encroach   encode   enlarge

6. We _____ the lost kitten in a warm blanket.

                increased   enfolded   engrossed

7. The children ran on the _____ snow without sinking their feet into it.

                enframed   encrusted   ingrained

Directions: Read the following words and their definitions. Then complete the rule.

word	definition
inflexible	not flexible
informal	not formal
innumerable	very many, not able to be counted
ineffective	not effective

● **In** is a prefix that can mean **cause to be** or **make.** The prefix **in** can also mean

_____.

Directions: Write each word from the first column on the line in front of its meaning in the second column.

entangled   _____   1.   put in a cage

inhale   _____   2.   breathe in

enchain   _____   3.   live in or on

enrobe   _____   4.   write on stone or paper

inhabit   _____   5.   fasten something in place with a chain

inscribe   _____   6.   get twisted and caught in

encage   _____   7.   add to or grow

increase   _____   8.   dress in a long, loose garment

Directions: Look closely at the pictures below to help you answer the questions. On the line beside each sentence, write the letter of the picture it describes.

 a.

 b.

 c.

 d.

 e.

_____ 1. Which one is *inscribing?*

_____ 2. Which one is *enrobed?*

_____ 3. Which one is *entangled?*

_____ 4. Which one is *encaged?*

_____ 5. Which one is *enchained?*

● **Mis** and **mal** are prefixes that usually mean **bad** or **badly**.

word	definition
misbehave	behave badly
maltreat	treat badly

Directions: Circle each word below in which **mis** or **mal** is used as a prefix.

mismatch	mallet	mister	maladjusted	misguide
mall	mislead	misuse	malformed	missing
misquote	misty	mistrust	malfunction	malpractice
missile	mistook	misdate	mission	misplace

Directions: Choose the word from the list below that best completes each sentence.

mispronounce	misdeal	malnutrition	misinformed	mistrust
malfunctioning	misfortune	misleading	misquoted	malformed

1. Uncle Dan's car made a loud noise. The noise was caused because the muffler was

    _____.

2. Pam dealt one player too many cards and another player too few cards. It was a

    _____.

3. The arrow on the sign pointed north, but it should have pointed east. The sign was

    _____.

4. Aggie enjoys being left-handed. She does not feel that being left-handed is a

    _____.

5. The leader made promises he never kept. Soon the followers began to

    _____ him.

6. Words in other languages often have different pronunciations than English words.

    Sometimes it is easy to _____ foreign words.

7. The little leaguer said, "I have two turtles." But the article _____ her by saying, "I hate two turtles."

8. Balanced meals provide good nutrition. "Junk food" can cause _____.

9. Marcie told Mark that the party was at 3:00, but it was actually at 2:00. Marcie

    _____ Mark.

10. My sister likes the cookies she bakes to look perfect. She lets me eat each one that is

    _____.

Directions: Rewrite each sentence below. Use the word in dark print to replace two words in each sentence.

1.	**misdated**	The check was incorrectly dated October 12.
2.	**malnutrition**	When they were found, the lost campers were suffering from bad diet.
3.	**misfortune**	Al had the bad luck of losing his homework.
4.	**mistreat**	Kind persons never treat other people badly.
5.	**misnamed**	It seems that the wild Pacific Ocean is wrongly named "peaceful."
6.	**mislabelled**	The shirt was incorrectly marked size 12.
7.	**misjudged**	Dressed alike, the two girls were wrongly judged as twins.
8.	**misused**	The bicycle didn't last long, because it was badly handled.
9.	**mistrial**	The judge declared an unfair trial, due to lack of evidence.
10.	**misbehave**	Children who are tired sometimes act badly.
11.	**maladjusted**	The jungle cat was badly adjusted to life in the zoo.
12.	**maladministered**	The club president ran the French club badly.

Directions: Read the title and story below. Circle each word that begins with a prefix. The prefixes to look for are **un, dis, ir, im, in, en, mis,** and **mal.** You should circle 25 words in all.

The Impossible Child

Helen Keller is a model of great courage. She had two major disabilities. She was blind and also deaf. Because she was unable to see and hear, she also became mute—not able to talk. Cut off entirely from the world, Helen was a maladjusted child. She misbehaved often, causing discord in her home. She acted irresponsibly, but her parents felt sorry for her. They thought she was incapable of improving her behavior.

Helen's parents became discouraged with their inability to help their unruly daughter. When she was seven, they sought help for her. Helen was entrusted to the insightful care of Anne Sullivan. Anne realized that Helen was not a stupid child. She did not pity her. She did not indulge her irresponsibility, as Helen's parents had done.

When she began enforcing rules, Anne had to endure Helen's rebellious actions. Patiently, Anne tried to talk with Helen through the sense of touch, spelling out words in the little girl's hand. Then came an unforgettable day! Helen realized that Anne was spelling the word *water* in her hand. From then on, Helen's progress was unbelievably rapid.

Far from being a misfit in society, Helen became famous for her wisdom and courage. She lived a full, enriching life. She has inspired countless disabled people to overcome their handicaps and to live life to the fullest.

Directions: Read each sentence. If the information is correct, write **yes.** If it is incorrect, write **no.**

1. Helen could see and hear, but not talk. _____

2. As a young child, Helen often behaved badly. _____

3. Helen's parents often punished her
   for her unruly behavior. _____

4. By the time Helen was seven, her parents were
   satisfied with the way she acted. _____

5. Anne Sullivan was often impatient with Helen. _____

6. Helen learned to lead a good, full life. _____

Directions: Two sentences can often be combined into one sentence for smoother writing. Combine each sentence pair below. Use the word in parentheses ( ) that you see below each pair as your connecting word. The first one is done for you.

1. Young Helen Keller was an unruly child. She became an inspiring adult.

    (but)

    Young Helen Keller was an unruly child, but she became an inspiring adult.

2. Helen Keller refused to feel disadvantaged. She did not let her handicaps keep her down.

    (and)

    _____

    _____

3. She even went to college. She graduated with honors.

    (and)

    _____

    _____

4. Helen was born with sight and hearing. An incurable disease destroyed these abilities when she was two.

    (but)

    _____

    _____

5. Helen wrote several books about her life. She wanted to encourage others who had disabilities.

    (because)

    _____

    _____

6. Helen needed help. Anne Sullivan came to stay in the Keller household.

    (so)

    _____

● **Pre** and **pro** are prefixes that usually mean **before**. **Pro** can also mean **forward**.

word	definition
precook	to cook before
proceed	to move ahead; go forward

Directions: Read each definition below. Choose a word from the list that fits it, and write the word on the line next to its definition.

preheat   prospective   promotion

preface   propel   prepay

1. _____ being put forward in rank

   _____

2. _____ something to happen in the future

   _____

3. _____ to drive forward; force ahead

   _____

4. _____ to heat before using

   _____

5. _____ introduction that comes before a book or speech

   _____

6. _____ give the money in advance

   _____

Directions: The sentences below are sample sentences for the definitions above. Choose the sentence that fits each meaning, and write it on the line below its meaning above.

1. The prospective buyer looked the house over carefully.

2. The recipe said to preheat the oven.

3. Our tickets to the game will be cheaper because we will prepay.

4. The young Indian can propel her canoe through the rapids with great skill.

5. Tim's dad received a promotion to office manager.

6. The preface to the mayor's speech was very long.

Directions: Read the comments in Column 1. Then answer the questions in column 2.

Column 1	Column 2

Column 1

1. **Fred:** "Oh, Kate, will you marry me?"
2. **Emily:** "I have a feeling that a bad storm is coming our way."
3. **Tess:** "I'll lock my bicycle."
4. **Bobby:** "I decided to stay in Mexico for another week."
5. **Nell:** "I'm sending in money now for the show next week."
6. **Andrea:** "No! It's not fair that I wash dishes again tonight!"

Column 2

1. Who is taking a precaution? _____

2. Who is proposing a marriage? _____

3. Who prolongs? _____

4. Who is prepaying for tickets? _____

5. Who has a premonition? _____

6. Who is protesting? _____

Directions: Follow the directions below.

1. Write a protest. _____

2. Make up a premonition. _____

3. Write something that would propel a friend into action. _____

_____

4. Tell about one precaution you or your family takes for safety. _____

_____

Directions: Read each meaning below. Then choose the word that best completes the sentence and circle it. Then write the word on the line.

● **Re** is a prefix that means **again** or **back.**

word	definition
recall	call to mind again
return	turn back

● **Ex** is a prefix that means **out of** or **from.**

word	definition
export	to send goods from a country
extend	to stretch out

1. **a leaving out:** I like all colors, with the _____ of pink.

   recapture   extreme   exception

2. **shut out; keep from entering:** Anyone who is not a U.S. citizen is _____ from becoming president.

   reclaimed   excluded   expected

3. **turned backward:** The _____ side of the record album has 6 songs.

   reverse   replay   excerpt

4. **on the outside; outer:** The _____ part of the cabin looked shabby, but inside it was cozy and warm.

   extreme   external   excitable

5. **pay back:** If you are not satisfied, the store will _____ your money.

   resell   reuse   refund

6. **put in place again:** Please _____ the book on the library shelf when you are finished reading it.

   research   expire   replace

7. **much more than usual; far out of the ordinary:** They felt _____ joy upon finding the lost hiker.

   extreme   excluded   reviewed

8. **bring back to confidence:** The pilot's steady voice _____ the passengers during the storm.

   rerouted   exclaimed   reassured

71

Directions: Circle each word below in which **re** is used as a prefix meaning **again.**

reassure	reading	rewash	ready	recall
refit	reconstruct	reclaim	reprint	reality
recapture	refresh	remedy	reap	redo
reason	rearrange	regal	rejoin	remarry
resident	recap	refuel	rebuild	register

Directions: Choose the word from the list below that best fits each meaning and sentence. Write the letters of the word in the boxes next to the sentence.

reorder   exhibit   reclaimed   respelling   excavate   exclaims   explosion

1. **speak out suddenly:** "I love sailing!" Joe _____ .

    ☐ ☐ ☐ ☐ ☐ ☐* ☐

2. **to get back again:** We _____ our lost puppy, Mugsy, at the dog pound.

    ☐ ☐ ☐ ☐ ☐* ☐ ☐ ☐

3. **spelling over again:** The students were judged after _____ several words.

    ☐ ☐ ☐ ☐ ☐ ☐ ☐ ☐* ☐ ☐

4. **a blowing up; outburst:** The _____ of the bomb caused great damage.

    ☐ ☐ ☐* ☐ ☐ ☐ ☐ ☐ ☐

5. **show; display:** The children _____ good manners. ☐ ☐ ☐ ☐ ☐ ☐* ☐

6. **request goods again:** She liked the dress so much that she decided to _____ another one.

    ☐ ☐ ☐ ☐* ☐ ☐ ☐

7. **dig out; make hollow:** They need to _____ a tunnel for the subway.

    ☐ ☐* ☐ ☐ ☐ ☐ ☐ ☐

Directions: To answer the riddle, write the letter under each star in order below.

Riddle: Which word has the most letters?

Answer: __ __ __ __ __ __

● **Fore** is a prefix that means **front** or **before.**

● **Post** is a prefix that means **after.**

word	definition
forehead	front of the head
postscript	a message written after a letter

Directions: Write the letter of each word on the line next to its meaning.

_____ 1. A time before noon   a. postdate

_____ 2. A date that comes after today   b. forearm

_____ 3. Give notice to danger before it happens   c. forecast

_____ 4. Generations after us; people of the future   d. posterity

_____ 5. An ability to see ahead and know about something before it happens   e. forenoon

_____ 6. To estimate what is coming before it happens   f. postpone

_____ 7. Front of the arm (between elbow and wrist)   g. foresight

_____ 8. Put off until later   h. forewarn

Directions: Now use a word from the list above to finish each sentence.

1. **Lifeguard:** "I _____ you against running near the pool because you could fall and get hurt."

2. **Citizen:** "We should not burn up all the oil in the world now, because what will _____ do?"

3. **Banker:** "Please don't _____ the check you are writing."

4. **Hostess:** "Because of the snowstorm, I'm going to _____ the garden party until next week."

5. **Piano teacher:** "Keep your _____ level with the keys while you play."

6. **Frustrated gardener:** "I wouldn't have sore hands now if I had had the _____ to bring along some gardening gloves."

7. **Restaurant owner:** "The _____ is our slowest time of day."

8. **Weatherwoman:** "I _____ bright, sunny skies for the weekend."

73

Directions: Answer each question with a word from the list. Then use the words to work the crossword puzzle below.

postpone	foresee	forepaws	postscript
postwar	forenoon	forecast	forehand
foreman	posterity	forehead	foretaste

Across

5. What is the person in charge of a work crew called?
8. What does a prophet supposedly do with the future?
10. What do the letters *P.S.* at the end of a letter stand for?
11. What period of the day is 11 o'clock in the morning?
12. What is the name of a type of stroke used in tennis?

Down

1. What are the front paws of an animal?
2. Who are the generations that live *after* us?
3. What does a weatherperson do?
4. What do hair bangs cover?
6. What is a sample of what is to come?
7. What do you call the period of time after war?
9. Which word means "put off an event until a later date"?

Directions: Read the story below. Circle each word that begins with one of these prefixes: **fore, ex, re, pre, pro.**

A Real American Princess

Matoaka was a real American princess. More often referred to as Pocahontas, Matoaka grew up in the wild expanse of what is now Virginia. It is not known exactly when she was born, because the Indians did not record births or deaths. Experts say she was born around the year 1595.

Her father, Powhatan, was one of the foremost chiefs in the region. He loved his daughter. He protected and provided for her. As a little girl, Pocahontas did the chores expected of her. She excelled in sewing and in making beads. Sometimes she had to restring the beads. Her mother provided excellent training.

One day when Pocahontas was exploring near the coast with some friends, she saw a huge ship. The men getting off this strange ship did not resemble Indians. Their faces were almost white. No one could have foreseen then that this group would establish the colony of Jamestown.

Chief Powhatan and his tribe expressed fear of these "palefaces." They soon captured the leader, Captain John Smith, and prepared to kill him. Pocahontas, then about 12 years old, protested when she saw the captain tied hand and foot. Her cries resounded throughout the village. She pleaded with her father to reconsider, but he pretended not to hear her. Pocahontas saw that she could not forestall Smith's death with tears or pleas. So just as they were about to kill Captain Smith, Pocahontas, with no forewarning, ran out and stood by him. If they killed him, they would have to kill her, too. Pocahontas exhibited great courage and preserved the life of John Smith. She and Captain Smith remained friends for as long as they lived.

Some years later, Pocahontas fell in love with a young Englishman named John Rolfe. When her father discovered that she wanted to marry an Englishman, he was angry. He did not approve of the match and hoped for a rematch with an Indian youth. But Powhatan could not prevent the wedding, and Pocahontas was married to John Rolfe. She and her husband went to England a few years later, so that Pocahontas could be presented to King James and Queen Anne. When she met them, they liked her and renamed her Lady Rebecca.

Directions: Write **true** or **false** on the line after each sentence below. Look back at the story on page 75 if you need to.

1. The real name of Pocahontas was Matoaka. _____

2. The Indians always wrote down the dates of births and deaths among their tribe. _____

3. Powhatan was a very important chief. _____

4. The men who came on the strange ship looked exactly like Indians. _____

5. Pocahontas was not very brave. _____

6. Powhatan saved John Smith because his daughter protested so loudly. _____

7. Pocahontas's mother gave her very good training. _____

8. Powhatan did not want his daughter to marry an Indian. _____

9. Powhatan was able to stop the wedding from taking place. _____

10. In England, Pocahontas was given the name of Lady Rebecca. _____

Directions: Two sentences can often be combined into one sentence for smoother writing. Combine each sentence pair below by using the word in parentheses ( ) as your connecting word.

1. John Rolfe proposed marriage to Pocahontas. Pocahontas accepted.   (and)

_____

_____

2. Powhatan did not approve of his daughter's marriage. John Rolfe was an Englishman.
(because)

_____

_____

3. Pocahontas married John Rolfe. She and Captain John Smith remained friends for life.
(but)

_____

_____

● When **over** is used as a prefix it means **too** or **too much.** You can tell the meaning of an adjective that begins with **over** by putting the word **too** in place of **over.**

overlong   overeager   overbold

● If a verb begins with **over,** the prefix **over** usually means **too much.**

overexercise   overspend   overheat

Directions: Choose the word that completes each sentence below. Write it on the line.

1. Grade five used the pencil sharpener so much that

   it broke from _____.   overuse   overflow

2. The children were _____ and couldn't sleep after the picnic.   overexcited   overripe

3. Doug talks for hours on the phone. He is

   _____.   overprecise   overtalkative

4. The apples must be eaten before they are

   _____.   overenormous   overripe

5. The team did not practice enough for the game

   because they were _____ about winning.   overconfident   overjealous

6. Mom said I made a very good meal because

   nothing was _____.   overspent   overcooked

7. Rebecca wears a hat at the beach because she is

   _____ to the sun.   overtired   oversensitive

8. Because the cake had too much sugar, it was

   _____.   oversweet   overserious

9. Ramón sometimes studies when he should be sleeping because he wants to be number one in

   school. His mom says he is _____.   overcrowded   overambitious

10. A woman who has spent more money than she

    earns has _____.   overgenerous   overspent

Directions: Choose the correct word to complete each sentence. Write the word on the line.

1. A(n) _____ parent will dress a child in warm clothes
                 protective   overprotective
   during cold winter weather.

2. Bill sent in $10.00 for the bat, but it only cost $9.99. Bill made a(n)

   _____ of one penny.
         payment   overpayment

3. A store that _____ its goods may soon lose its customers.
                   prices   overprices

4. The athlete was healthy and fit from _____ every day.
                         exercising   overexercising

5. The bananas were mushy and black because they were

   _____.
         ripe   overripe

6. Pamela thinks that playing games is a waste of time. Pamela seems to be

   _____.
         serious   overserious

7. A pet that is _____ will become fat.
               fed   overfed

8. I did not have much money, so I was careful not to _____
                         spend   overspend
   at the fair.

9. The countryside is _____ with just a few farms.
               populated   overpopulated

10. Someone whose hopes are too high could be called

    _____.
          optimistic   overoptimistic

● **Co, com,** and **con** are prefixes that mean **with** or **together.**

word	definition
cooperate	to work with others
combine	to join together or unite
conspire	to plan secretly with others to do something wrong

Directions: Add the prefix **co, com,** or **con** to each word and root below. The word you make should fit the definition.

1. _____pete: take part in a contest with others

2. _____tagious: easily spreading from one to another

3. _____operation: working together; a united effort

4. _____-star: a leading actor appearing with another star in the same production

5. _____pany: people grouped together such as guests or visitors

Directions: Now use the words you made above. Write the word on the line that correctly completes each sentence.

1. Winning a basketball game takes team _____.

2. Measles is a _____ disease.

3. Did your school _____ with Southdale School in soccer?

4. My family is entertaining _____ for the holiday.

5. My favorite actor will _____ with Wanda Wonderful in the new film Computers in Space.

79

Directions: Choose a word from the list to complete each unfinished sentence.

Prefix co

coincide   coeducation   cooperate   coincidence

1. Some private schools teach only boys or only girls. They do not have

   _____.

2. The two friends had not planned to meet, but by _____ they approached the same store clerk at the same time.

3. Two people who _____ together can get more done than one person working alone.

4. Josh and Jim rarely see each other because their leisure hours don't

   _____.

Prefix com

commence   companion   compose   common

1. The people who live in these houses share a _____ park.

2. Another word for <u>begin</u> or <u>start</u> is _____.

3. A synonym for a <u>friend</u> is _____.

4. When you put together a story in your own words, you _____ it.

Prefix con

consecutive   conserve   conquer   consoled

1. A bad habit is difficult to _____.

2. Someone who is sad or distressed may need to be _____.

3. One, two, three, and four are _____ numbers.

4. By turning off lights, we help _____ electricity.

● **Sub** can mean **under, below,** or **not quite.** A **subway** train travels under the ground. **Mid** can mean the **middle part. Midnight** is the middle of the night.

Directions: Read each definition. Then add the prefix **mid** or **sub** to the beginning of the word to make a word that fits the definition.

1. a ship that goes under sea: _____marine

2. halfway; in the middle: _____way

3. put down or overcome by superior force; conquer: _____due

4. a person below another in rank: _____ordinate

5. air above the ground; in the middle of the air: _____air

6. existing below the conscious; not fully recognized in the mind: _____conscious

7. middle of the week; Wednesday: _____week

8. middle of a stream: _____stream

Directions: Follow the directions to finish the picture in the box below.

1. Draw a **submarine** in **midocean.**
2. Draw a jogger who is **midway** over the bridge.
3. Draw a large fish in **midstream.**
4. Draw an airplane in **midair.**

Directions: Answer each question by circling the correct answer.

1. Which day occurs **midweek?**

   Sunday   Friday   Wednesday

2. Which animal would you look for in **midstream?**

   robin   mouse   fish

3. Which of these travels **underwater?**

   ship   submarine   subway train

4. Which one is **subservient?**

   king   servant   ruler

5. When is **midday?**

   noon   10 a.m.   2 p.m.

6. Which one is in the **midriff** area?

   leg   neck   waistline

7. Which one earns **substandard** living?

   wealthy queen   middle-class person   poor peasant

8. Which color is **subtle?**

   dark red   bright orange   light lavender

9. When is **midnight?**

   twelve o'clock at night   10 o'clock at night   6 o'clock at night

10. Which word is an antonym of **subtract?**

    divide   add   multiply

11. What happens to a storm that **subsides?**

    It dies down.   It causes damage.   It gets stronger.

12. What is the **subscript** in the formula H_2O?

    H   2   O

● **Bi** and **tri** are prefixes. **Bi** means **two. Tri** means **three.**
A **bicycle** has two wheels. A **tripod** has three legs.

Directions: Choose the word from the list that describes each picture, and write it on the line. Use your dictionary if you need to.

| bifocals | triangle | biplane | biceps |
| trio | binoculars | triple-dip | tripod |

_____

_____

_____

_____

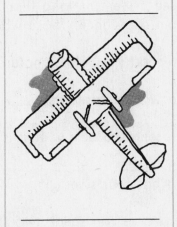

_____

_____

_____

_____

Directions: Use each word from the list in a sentence of your own.

1. bifocals _____

2. trio _____

3. biceps _____

4. triangle _____

5. binoculars _____

6. tripod _____

7. biplane _____

8. triple-dip _____

83

Directions: Complete the following story by using a word from the list to complete each unfinished sentence. There is one word you will not use.

binoculars	triplets	Bicentennial	tricolored
Tricentennial	bifocals	bicultural	tricycles

On July 4, 1976, America became 200 years old. It was the biggest and best

birthday party Americans had ever seen—the Great _____.

For weeks before the big day, people splashed red, white, and blue paint all over

America. Some children painted each wheel of their _____ with one of the

three patriotic colors. On the day itself, one set of _____ paraded in New

York, each one dressed in a flag color. One man even sported a _____
beard!

The original Declaration of Independence was shown in Washington, D. C. The lines

of people waiting to see it were so long that some people used _____ to
view the document from a distance. Those who got close did not need to wear

_____ to read the bold signature of John Hancock!

In 2076, America will celebrate its _____. How old will you be?

Directions: Read each sentence below. If it is correct, write **true.** If it is incorrect, write **false.**

1. _____ A **triangle** has four sides.

2. _____ **Bilingual** people can speak two languages.

3. _____ A **bimonthly** magazine comes out every week.

4. _____ A set of **triplets** has one child more

   than a set of twins.

5. _____ The U.S. flag is **bicolored.**

6. _____ Mexican-Americans often have

   bicultural life-styles.

Directions: Read the story below. Circle each word that begins with one of these prefixes: **over, bi, tri, sub, mid, con, co, com.**

Willie Mays

Willie Mays was one of baseball's superstars. He contracted to play with the New York Giants in 1950, when he was only nineteen years old. This made Willie the second black person to be admitted to major league baseball. The first person to make the game of baseball biracial had been Jackie Robinson, three years before. Never one to be overconfident, Willie felt at first that he could not compete well enough to be in a major league. At midseason of his first year, his batting record was poor. But the manager helped Willie conquer his fears by telling him that he was overanxious and should not worry so much. The manager said that he would not send such a fine player as Willie back to the minors.

It may have been the most commendable decision ever made by the manager. Willie went on to subject opposing teams to defeat after defeat. He had an outstanding combination of baseball talents.

His coequal, Joe DiMaggio, made this comment about Mays: "This man does it all. He hits, he fields, he runs, he studies, he hardly ever make mistakes."

Mays hit plenty of singles, doubles, and triples. But he is especially remembered for the long list of home runs he compiled—660 in all. In the 1954 World Series, Willie made one overhead catch in midair while on the run. It is considered one of the most outstanding plays in baseball history.

Directions: Answer each question about the story by writing **yes** or **no.**

_____ 1. Did Willie sign a major league contract when he was 19 years old?

_____ 2. Was Willie the first black man to play for the major leagues?

_____ 3. Was Willie at first unsure of his own ability?

_____ 4. Had Willie compiled a superb batting record by the middle of his first year in the major leagues?

_____ 5. Did Willie have several baseball talents?

_____ 6. Does the writer of this story seem to think that Willie was superior in baseball to Joe DiMaggio?

_____ 7. Did Willie dive to capture a ground-ball in his famous catch of 1954?

85

Directions: Two sentences can often be combined into one sentence for smoother writing. Combine each pair of sentences below. Use the word in parentheses as your connecting word.

1. At one time, no black people played for the major leagues. Jackie Robinson broke the racial barrier. (but)

_____

_____

2. The Giants at first paid Willie $5,000. They later gave him a $100,000 contract. (however)

_____

_____

3. Willie's dad was a semipro baseball player. Will was "brought up" on the game. (so)

_____

_____

Directions: Combine each sentence pair below using your own connecting word. You may wish to use one of the connecting words used above.

1. Willie Mays, the solid superstar, was five feet, eleven inches tall. He weighed one hundred eighty-five pounds.

_____

_____

2. Willie played for the Giants during most of his career. He was traded to the Mets in 1972.

_____

_____

_____

_____

● A **root** is a word or word part to which prefixes and suffixes can be added to make new words. Knowing the meanings of certain word parts can often help you figure out the meaning of a new word. Here are some roots, or word parts:

pos usually means **put** or **place** (position)

pel or **pul** usually means **push, drive,** or **thrust** (propel)

Directions: Read the sentences and underline the words that contain the roots **pos, pel** or **pul.**

1. The noise of the helicopter's propeller drowned out our voices.
2. Are you positive our unexpected visit will not be an imposition?
3. The girl's nightmares were dispelled when her fever went down.
4. A good way to dispose of your litter is to deposit it in a trash can.
5. The doctor took the patient's pulse.
6. Please stand up straight to keep good posture.
7. The huge plane moved across the sky by jet propulsion.
8. Can you play this new composition on the piano?

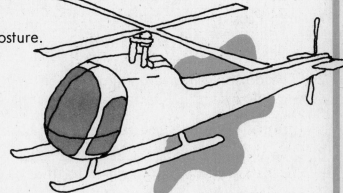

Directions: Write the number of each word on the line beside its definition.

1. propellers _____ driven away
2. dispelled _____ a driving force
3. imposition _____ revolving blades that move an aircraft
4. propulsion _____ heartbeat felt as blood is pushed through the arteries
5. pulse _____ a burden, something placed on another

1. positive _____ to put in a safe place
2. dispose _____ position of the body
3. deposit _____ certain of one's position
4. posture _____ words or music that is placed on paper
5. composition _____ get rid of, put away from

87

● Here are some other roots, or word parts.

port means **carry** (portable)
ject means **throw** or **force** (eject)

Directions: Read the words below. Underline each word in which you see the root **port.** Circle each word in which you see the root **ject.**

portfolio	important	reporter
injection	transporting	rejection
export	ejector	adjectives
subjects	porter	projector

Directions: Read each unfinished sentence. Choose the word from the list above that matches the definition below the line. Write the word on the line to complete the sentence.

1. The ferry is _____ the motorcycle to the island.
   (carrying across)

2. The doctor will give my grandpa his yearly _____ against
   (shot, fluid forced into)
   the flu.

3. We will need the _____ to show this wildlife film.
   (machine for throwing light)

4. Which products does Canada _____ to Africa?
   (carry out, send out)

5. In case of emergency the plane that the test pilot flies always has an

   _____ seat.
   (thing that throws out)

6. I was disappointed when the photo I took got a

   _____ from the magazine.
   (notice of refusal, something thrown back)

7. We will need to find a _____ when we get to the hotel.
   (someone who carries luggage)

8. I plan to show my _____ of cartoons to
   (collection of papers that can be carried around)
   my friend Jim.

9. The television _____ went to cover the fire.
   (person who carries back a story)

● Look at these roots, or word parts.

aud means **hear** (<u>aud</u>ience)
dict usually means **tell** or **say** (<u>dict</u>ation)

Directions: Find the word in the list that matches the definition below the line in each sentence. Then write the word on the line.

dictation	audible	dirigible	audio-visual
awful	diphthong	auditorium	direction
audition	auction	dictionary	predict

1. Will you buy me a new _____ when I go back to school?
   (book that tells about words)

2. Is the movie in the school _____?
   (place where people hear or see something)

3. Please speak up because your voice is barely _____ over the phone.
   (able to be heard)

4. I'm going to _____ for the drama club.
   (try out, have a hearing)

5. The boss called her secretary in to take some _____.
   (words said aloud to be copied)

6. The science teacher showed us _____ materials
   (materials that can be heard and seen)

   on snakes.

Directions: Circle the word that correctly completes each sentence, and write it on the line.

1. A ruler who has power over everybody in a country is a _____.

   predictor   dictator   valedictorian

2. A group of people gathered to hear and see something is an _____.

   audience   audible   audiometer

3. To say something that is opposite of what someone else has said is to

   _____.

   contravene   contraband   contradict

89

● Look at these roots, or word parts, and their meanings.

duct or **duce** usually means **lead** (con<u>duct</u>)
scribe or **script** means **write** or **something written** (in<u>scribe</u>)

Now look at these prefixes and their meanings. You may already know some of them.

intro means **in**   **sub** means **under**   **con** means **together**
de means **down, away from**   **e** means **from**

Directions: Read each word in the list. Draw a line under the prefix. Then circle the root in each word.

conductor	deduct	introduce
reduced	subscribe	description
education	describe	inscription

Directions: Use a word from the list above to complete each unfinished sentence. The roots and prefixes will help you figure out the correct word. You will not use all the words.

1. This word means "to bring or lead something new into a place." For example, club members can bring up new business to be discussed at a meeting. The word also

   means "to present one person to another." The word is _____.

2. When people used to buy magazines, they would have to sign their name on a contract. That is, they would "write their names under" the agreement. Today the

   word meaning "to buy magazines" is _____.

3. This word means "to subtract," or "to lead away." For example, if you broke a

   window, you might have to _____ the cost from your weekly allowance.

4. This word can mean "to write down something in detail." But we usually use it to mean "to tell about something." Your teacher might ask you to

   _____ your summer vacation.

5. This word describes a system of learning. It means "the process of leading, or

   drawing out of." We call it _____.

6. This word means "something written in." Perhaps you want a friend to write something in your yearbook or autograph book. It would be called an

   _____.

7. This word means "someone who leads or guides the members of a group." The word

   is _____.

● Read these roots, or word parts, and their meanings.

spec or **spect** means **see, look,** or **examine** (in<u>spect</u>)
mit or **miss** means **send** or **let go** (ad<u>mit</u>)

Directions: Read the sentences and underline the words that contain the roots **spec, spect, mit,** or **miss.**

1. Melissa made quite a spectacle of herself when she asked for a raise in her allowance.
2. Mom signed the note to show I was permitted to go on the class trip.
3. What day will we be dismissed for summer vacation?
4. The prospector made a mistake when he drew a map to show where he had discovered the gold mine.
5. The suspect will be questioned by the police.
6. I'll meet you near the popcorn stand during the movie intermission.
7. The spy was sent on a top-secret mission.
8. The spectators cheered as the final seconds of the game ticked away.

Directions: Write the number of each word beside its meaning.

1. spectacle _____ a period between acts when people go out of the theater

2. permit _____ a person who looks for something

3. dismiss _____ a display, something to look at

4. prospector _____ a job, assignment that a person is sent on

5. expect _____ to let go or send away

6. intermission _____ to look or wait for

7. mission _____ to let or allow

8. spectators _____ people who watch or look at something

● Here are some more roots, or word parts, and their meanings.

fac/fect/fic/feit mean **do, make,** or **cause** (<u>fac</u>tory)

Directions: Read the words below. Circle the root **fac, fect, fic,** or **feit** in each word.

defective	facsimile	difficult
factory	counterfeit	benefactor
fiction	effect	perfect

Directions: Use the words in the list to work the crossword puzzle below.

Down

1. having a problem or weakness
4. piece of writing about something made-up
5. something fake intended to fool people

Across

1. hard to do
2. place where things can be made
3. person who does something kind or good
4. an imitation or exact copy
6. result; something caused by something else
7. without a mistake

92

Directions: Below is a list of words that have roots that you have studied in this unit. Read the words and then read the story. Choose the correct word from the list to complete each sentence, and write it on the line. Use your dictionary if you need to.

audibly	reporter	defective
position	projector	ejector
audience	contradict	received

Miss Carl was leaving her teaching _____ to become a
                                                    1

_____ for the *Suburban Times*. Her fifth-grade class wanted to surprise her.
         2

They wanted to do something different.

"Let's have a piñata party." suggested Carlos.

"I don't like to _____ your suggestion, Carlos," said Lisa, "but we
                                   3

had one at Christmas."

"We could have a slide show," said Heidi.

Everyone liked Heidi's idea. They decided to invite the other fifth-grade class so that

they would have an _____. Bill was sure his brother would let them use
                                    4

the slide _____ he had just _____ for his birthday.
                      5   6

When Bill tried to use it, the slides wouldn't drop down and pop up the way they

were supposed to. There was something wrong with the _____.
                                                                              7

Fortunately, Bill quickly found the _____ part and replaced it with a
                                                      8

new one.

The party was a huge success. Miss Carl was so surprised when she saw the slide

show that she gasped _____.
                                 9

"Thank you," she said. "You are a wonderful class! I will always remember you!"

93

When you write a paragraph, all the information in the paragraph should be about the same thing. The main idea sentence tells what the paragraph is about. It can be found anywhere in the paragraph. All the other sentences should give details about the main idea.

Directions: Read the following paragraph. Choose the sentence that tells the main idea of the paragraph.

Last night I had to forfeit my chance to play basketball. I was a mere spectator. How dejected I felt! My foot had gotten infected, and my doctor would not permit me to play. It was hard being submissive to the doctor's orders.

Write the main idea sentence here.

_____

Now reread the paragraph, and circle each word that has a root that you have learned about in this unit. Write the words on the lines below.

_____ _____

_____ _____

_____ _____

● A **compound word** is made up of two or more other words. Each word in a compound word can stand alone and still have meaning.

$$cupcake = cup + cake$$

$$snowstorm = snow + storm$$

Directions: Read each sentence and underline each compound word. Be sure that the words you underline are made up of two words that can stand on their own.

1. Which insect did you see after sunset, a firefly or a ladybug?

2. How many payments has your grandfather made on this typewriter?

3. The blacksmith hammered away at the bent horseshoe.

4. The undersea earthquake caused a tidal wave.

5. Does your grandmother have a remedy for a toothache?

6. My little sister wore her snowsuit when she played in the snowdrifts.

7. The ranger could see the waterfall from her lookout.

8. They are sending an icebreaker to rescue the steamship.

9. We listened to the television broadcast of the countdown for the spaceship launch.

10. Julie will be without a car until Sunday since the gearshift needs an overhaul.

Directions: Find the correct compound word from those you underlined above to match each definition below. Write the word on the line.

1. strong shaking of the earth's surface

   _____

2. beginning of night

   _____

3. to completely fix or redo

   _____

4. a machine that can make printed letters on paper

   _____

5. a vehicle used to travel in outer space

   _____

95

Directions: Write each word in the first column next to the word it can go with to make a compound word. Then write each compound word you made under the correct heading below.

1		2	1		2	1		2
grape	_____	bread	cat	_____	coat	pan	_____	fish
earth	_____	fly	over	_____	meal	pea	_____	shirt
blue	_____	fruit	neck	_____	socks	sweat	_____	links
corn	_____	bird	knee	_____	fish	star	_____	cakes
horse	_____	worm	oat	_____	tie	cuff	_____	nut

Kinds of food

1. _____
2. _____
3. _____
4. _____
5. _____

Kinds of animals

1. _____
2. _____
3. _____
4. _____
5. _____

Things to wear

1. _____
2. _____
3. _____
4. _____
5. _____

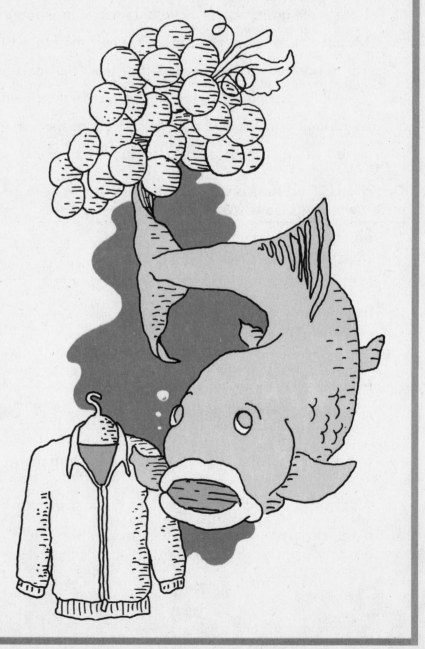

The letter **s** with a mark before it—like this **'s**—is called **apostrophe s.** The mark is an apostrophe. The **'s** is added to a word to show that someone or something owns, has, or possesses something. For example:

Ella has a skateboard.   This is Ella's skateboard.

The **'s** after the word Ella shows that Ella owns or has a skateboard.
Here are some other examples:

the baby's rattle   the car's engine   Joseph's book

Directions: Read each sentence below. Then circle the word at the right that correctly completes the sentence. Write the word on the line. Reread the information above if you need to.

1. The _____ windows were covered with ice after the storm.   cars   car's

2. Several _____ galloped through the pasture.   horses   horse's

3. _____ bike was repainted last week.   Randys   Randy's

4. The _____ loud jangling ring woke me up.   telephones   telephone's

5. Are the _____ coming for dinner today?   Smiths   Smith's

6. The _____ throw missed third base by a mile.   outfielders   outfielder's

7. The _____ windup seemed to take forever.   pitchers   pitcher's

8. Where are the six pairs of _____ I left on the counter?   socks   sock's

9. The science project took me one _____ time to finish.   months   month's

10. The _____ legs gave out just after she won the race.   runners   runner's

11. We were amazed at the size of the

_____ ears.   elephants   elephant's

12. The _____ at the zoo were larger than we expected, too.   anteaters   anteater's

13. The _____ in the snow led to the frozen pond.   footprints   footprint's

97

● To make a singular noun show possession, **add apostrophe s.**
   Sally's coat

● To make a plural noun ending in **s** show possession, just add an **apostrophe.**
   the boots' zippers

● To make a plural noun not ending in **s** show possession, add **apostrophe s.**
   the children's skateboards

Directions: Read each sentence below. Write the correct possessive form of the word that you see below the line. Look back at the rules if you need to.

1. Stan rolled down the _____ window because the afternoon sun
    car

    was hot.

2. The store is having a sale on _____ shoes.
    women

3. Will you help me plan _____ birthday party?
    Elena

4. The _____ tires were flat.
    bicycle

5. The _____ orbits carry them around the sun.
    planets

6. The _____ cage needed cleaning.
    mice

7. The _____ side was covered with lava.
    volcano

8. I'm afraid these _____ roots are badly damaged.
    vegetables

9. The sound of thousands of _____ wings filled the air in the cave.
    bats

10. Horace hoped to break the champion _____ record.
    swimmer

11. Do you know where I can find the _____ clothing department?
    men

12. The _____ flap did not stay sealed.
    envelope

LESSON 37: UNDERSTANDING CONTRACTIONS

● A **contraction** is a short way of writing two words. The two words are written together but one or more letters have been left out. An apostrophe stands for the missing letters.

it is = it's (the letter **i** has been left out)
I will = I'll (the letters **wi** have been left out)

Directions: Read the words in the first column. Find the contraction in the second column that stands for the two words. Write the words on the line beside their contraction. Then in the box write the letter or letters that the apostrophe stands for.

1		**2**	
we are	_____	they'll	☐
did not	_____	wouldn't	☐
I am	_____	we're	☐
we will	_____	you're	☐
would not	_____	it's	☐
they will	_____	I'm	☐
you are	_____	didn't	☐
it is	_____	we'll	☐
I have	_____	I've	☐

1		**2**	
she will	_____	can't	☐
you have	_____	isn't	☐
is not	_____	she'll	☐
let us	_____	let's	☐
he is	_____	that's	☐
can not	_____	Sandy's	☐
Sandy is	_____	you've	☐
that is	_____	he's	☐

99

Directions: Read the story and underline each contraction. On a line at the bottom of the page write the two words that each contraction stands for.

Sara climbed out of bed grumbling to herself. "I don't believe it! The one day I have to be up early, my alarm clock doesn't go off. If Henry had anything to do with this, I'll have something to say to him!"

She stumbled into her clothes, still half asleep. Her shoes didn't fit, and she realized she hadn't put them on the right feet. "Let's get this together," she muttered. "I'm not going to miss the last day of the spelling contest. Nancy's going to be at school early. I know she'll be there before anybody else so she can get some extra study time."

Finally Sara was ready. She raced down the stairs, not even stopping to grab the book she was reading. As she ran outside she bumped into her brother Henry on the porch.

"What kept you?" he asked.

"My alarm clock didn't go off."

"I hope I wasn't at fault. I set it last night so it would go off early," Henry explained. "At least that's what I thought I did."

"Well, you've got a lot to learn about clocks," said Sara. "Come on, or we'll both be late."

1. _____

2. _____

3. _____

4. _____

5. _____

6. _____

7. _____

8. _____

9. _____

10. _____

11. _____

12. _____

13. _____

14. _____

- A word has as many syllables as it has vowel sounds.

- A prefix is a syllable in itself if it contains a vowel sound. Divide the word between the prefix and the root word. Some prefixes have more than one syllable.

Directions: Decide how many syllables each word below contains. Write the number of syllables on the first line. Then divide the word into syllables, using vertical lines.

1. dispose _____ _____   13. transport _____ _____

2. subject _____ _____   14. dictation _____ _____

3. predict _____ _____   15. subscribe _____ _____

4. audible _____ _____   16. mission _____ _____

5. introduce _____ _____   17. counterfeit _____ _____

6. reduce _____ _____   18. perfect _____ _____

7. permit _____ _____   19. deceive _____ _____

8. spectator _____ _____   20. expect _____ _____

9. defect _____ _____   21. conduct _____ _____

10. posture _____ _____   22. reporter _____ _____

11. subdivide _____ _____   23. postscript _____ _____

12. biennial _____ _____   24. submerge _____ _____

Directions: Read each sentence, find the missing word, and write it on the line.

1. Mom said I could _____ to the magazine for the summer. subscribe / subject

2. The news _____ interviewed the girl who saved the drowning child. reporter / spectator

Here are some other rules about syllabication.

● When you divide compound words:
  <u>First</u>, divide the word between the smaller words that make up the compound word.
  <u>Second</u>, divide the smaller words into syllables if this is necessary.

peanut	**pea|nut**	
underground	**under|ground**	**un|der|ground**

Directions: Divide each compound word into syllables, using vertical lines. For the words that need it, you can go through the two steps above.

1. seashore _____
2. mailbox _____
3. skyscraper _____
4. overcoat _____
5. workbook _____
6. watermelon _____
7. wristwatch _____
8. anteater _____
9. buttonhole _____
10. grandparent _____
11. somebody _____

12. sailboat _____
13. strawberry _____
14. newspaper _____
15. beehive _____
16. haystack _____
17. quicksand _____
18. fingerprint _____
19. ladybug _____
20. clothespin _____
21. windmill _____
22. workshop _____

Directions: Read each sentence, find the missing word, and write it on the line.

1. On our vacation we collected shells at the _____.

   seashore
   quicksand

2. Linda and her friends brought _____ for dessert to their picnic.

   watermelon
   anteater

Directions: Read the contractions, possessives, and compound words in the list below. Then write the correct word from the list in each blank to complete the sentences.

ladybug's	He'll	doesn't	it's	there's
she'd	spiderweb	Katie's	volleyball	hummingbirds
butterfly	anteaters	earthworms	notebook	I'm

The people in my family are crazy about animals. _____ most

1

interested in animals that fly. Katie is my sister. Yesterday she said _____

                                                 2

seen two _____ and a swallowtail _____ on her way

               3   4

to _____ practice. Then _____ Ricky, my brother. His

      5   6

favorite creatures are crawling things, like insects and _____. He

                                              7

_____ collect them to bring home. He just watches them and writes

     8

down things in his _____. He especially likes the _____

                 9   10

red spots. _____ always stop for hours to observe a spider spin a

        11

_____ just to see how _____ done. Now

     12   13

_____ more sensible. I especially like animals with long snouts, such as

     14

elephants and _____.

                 15

Directions: Read the following sentences. Decide which one states the main idea of the paragraph and write **MI** next to it. Figure out which two are supporting details and write **SD** next to each. Put an **X** next to the sentence that does not say anything about the paragraph.

_____ The writer's friend does not like animals at all.

_____ The writer's brother watches spiders spin webs.

_____ The writer likes animals with long snouts.

_____ The writer's family enjoys watching animals.

Directions: Complete each sentence by using one of the words from the list.

apostrophe   contraction   possessive
syllables   compound

1. A _____ is a short way of writing two words.

2. An _____ stands for the letter or letters that are missing.

3. A _____ form shows that someone or something owns, has, or possesses something.

4. A _____ word is made up of two smaller words that can stand alone.

5. There are many rules for dividing words into parts.

   Word parts are called _____.

Directions: Divide each of the words in the list above into syllables on the lines below. Use vertical lines when you divide each word.

1. _____   4. _____

2. _____   5. _____

3. _____

Directions: Write two sentences about the apostrophe. Write about the different ways it is used. In your sentences try to use a contraction and a possessive. Also see if you can include a compound word.

_____

_____

_____

_____

_____

_____

_____

_____

● A suffix is a word part added to the end of a root. It always changes the meaning of the root in some way.

● The suffixes **er** and **or** mean **someone who does something**, or **a thing that can do something.** These suffixes can change a verb into a noun.

verb	noun
bake	baker
project	projector

● The suffix **ist** also can mean **someone who does something.** But it changes one kind of noun into another kind of noun.

noun	noun
science	scientist

Directions: Add **er** or **or** to each verb to make a noun. If a word ends with an **e,** drop the **e** before adding the suffix.

-er

1. write _____
2. train _____
3. interpret _____
4. paint _____
5. labor _____

-or

6. act _____
7. inspect _____
8. visit _____
9. counsel _____
10. edit _____

Directions: Add **ist** to each root to make another word. If the root ends in **y,** drop the **y** before adding **ist.**

1. ideal _____
2. archaeology _____
3. novel _____
4. cartoon _____
5. optometry _____
6. real _____

Directions: Use one of the words you made in the above exercises to complete each sentence below.

1. The drama critics gave the _____ in the new play good reviews.

2. The horse's _____ refused to run him on a lame leg.

3. The newspaper printed a funny drawing by its famous _____.

4. My sister will go to the _____ to have her eyes checked.

105

● The suffixes **er** and **est** are added to adjectives to make them show comparison.

Today is **hot.**
Today is **hotter** than yesterday. (Two days are being compared.)
Today is the **hottest** day of the summer. (More than two days are being compared.)

Directions: Read each sentence and the two words under the line. Choose the word that completes the sentence and write it on the line.

1. These apples are _____ than those we had last week.
   sweeter   sweetest

2. The comedian is so _____ that people can't stop laughing.
   funny   funnier

3. This is the _____ party I've ever had.
   noisy   noisiest

4. Have you ever seen such a _____ day?
   dreary   dreariest

5. The film was _____ at the end than at the beginning.
   scarier   scariest

6. Leave it to Jane to pick the _____ path.
   muddy   muddiest

7. The cat's eyes are very _____ in the soft light.
   bright   brightest

8. Of the two cities, Darwell is the _____.
   colder   coldest

9. Jan is a _____ person with a wisecrack.
   quick   quicker

10. Hal always acts _____ than everyone else.
    smarter   smartest

11. This stuffed animal is the

    _____ one I have ever seen.
    fuzzier   fuzziest

Directions: Read the words above each paragraph. Use them to complete the sentences.

dirty   dirtier   dirtiest

1. We were washing our _____ car. The inside windows were the

_____ parts on the whole car. But the hubcaps were

_____ than they had been the last time we washed them.

large   larger   largest

2. The sales clerk showed me some _____ sweaters to give for the

present. They were _____ than the ones I had at home. In fact they

were the _____ sweaters in the store.

hungry   hungrier   hungriest

3. Tad is the _____ boy I have ever known.

He is usually _____ at dinner than he was at lunch.

But then, he is _____ most of the time.

weak   weaker   weakest

4. The radio signals grew _____ as the evening wore on. They had

been quite _____ when the storm began. But they were the

_____ during the heaviest thunder and lightning.

early   earlier   earliest

5. José gets up the _____ of anyone in our class. Morrie thinks he

gets up _____ , but even I get up _____ than he does.

● The suffix **eer** usually means **someone who.**

word	definition
auctioneer	someone who is in charge of an auction

● The suffixes **ee, ent,** and **ant** can also mean **someone who.** These suffixes can also mean **that which.**

word	definition
employee	someone who is employed
repellent	that which repels

Directions: Read the list of words below. Choose the word that matches each definition and write it on the blank next to the definition. You will not use all the words.

auction	appointee	auctioneer	occupant
absentee	accounts	accountant	assistant
descendant	occupies	payee	payer
dependent	engineer	superintendent	electioneer

1. one who runs a school system   _____

2. one who is not present   _____

3. one who lives somewhere   _____

4. one who has a family history   _____

5. one who runs elections   _____

6. one who works with engines   _____

7. one who receives pay   _____

8. one who depends on someone else   _____

9. one who works with numbers and figures _____

10. one who helps someone else   _____

11. one who is appointed   _____

Directions: Look at each sentence or pair of sentences below and the two words at the right. Write the words on the lines to complete each sentence.

1. We need a good _____ to _____ us on
   European travel.   (inform, informant)

2. The _____ rounded the corner on two wheels, but the

   _____ brought it under control.   (chariot, charioteer)

3. You cannot just _____ the problem. You may act

   _____ , but it will not just go away.   (ignore, ignorant)

4. Which _____ did you hire last? How many did you

   _____ all month?   (employ, employee)

5. This is one of the oldest _____ hotels in the city. Many people

   _____ here.   (reside, resident)

6. This cloth is not very _____. We better find a towel to

   _____ the spilled milk.   (absorb, absorbent)

7. The company needs a dependable _____ to

   _____ the manager.   (assist, assistant)

8. Our letter came back stamped "_____ unknown." Where can we

   find the Dentons' _____?   (addressee, address)

9. The spray's smell really _____ me. So I'm sure it will be a good

   _____ for the insects.   (repels, repellent)

10. The _____ looked up at the peak. Then she shouldered her pack

    and started up the _____.   (mountain, mountaineer)

11. You are a very _____ person. You always _____
    until you get your way.   (persist, persistent)

12. The _____ was very nervous before the _____
    on the TV show began.   (contest, contestant)

Directions: Read each sentence and the question that follows it. Answer the question by forming a new word from the root word and the suffix **ward, en,** or **ize.** Write the new word on the line.

1. When the guests had gone, Art cleaned up the dishes.
    When did Art clean up?

    after _____

2. Ellie knitted her sister some warm socks.
    What kind of socks were they?

    wool _____

3. I opened the cage to let the wild bird loose.
    Which way did the bird fly?

    sky _____

4. Joanie was looking for a book title in the card catalog.
    What did Joanie have to do?

    alphabet _____

5. "If I pull my belt another notch, maybe I won't be so hungry," joked Sam.
    What did Sam want to do to his belt?

    tight _____

6. The mound was made of clay, mud, and dirt.
    What kind of mound was it?

    earth _____

7. Mr. and Mrs. Thomas redecorated their apartment according to the latest style.
    What did Mr. and Mrs. Thomas do to their apartment?

    modern _____

Look at the suffixes and their meanings below.

ful (adjective)	full of or having a tendency to	**cheerful, careful**
ful (noun)	a certain amount	**handful, scoopful**
ness	quality or condition of being	**newness, happiness**

Directions: Read the list of words below. Then choose one to complete each sentence. Write the correct word on the line.

useful	weakness	loudness	successful
wildness	faithful	peaceful	dryness
harmful	plentiful	friendliness	spoonful

1. Anne and Marti started a craft shop that became quite _____.

2. Pat could feel the _____ in his mouth as he crept through the cold, dark tunnel.

3. Sam and Keith were _____ friends for many years.

4. We could not get over the _____ of the woods where we camped.

5. Flowers were _____ in the desert after the rains, but they disappeared during the drought.

6. Horace fed his baby sister by the _____.

7. Please put these _____ pesticides where the children won't be able to reach them.

8. Can you adjust the _____ on the TV set so Howie can hear it in the kitchen?

9. Ginger is over the flu, but she still suffers from _____.

10. After hearing the yelling and cheering at the basketball game, the drive home was very _____.

11. His pals think the best characteristic about Ted is his _____.

12. I hope this library book will be _____ to you.

111

Directions: Choose the word that best completes each sentence and write it on the line.

1. The puppet show _____ Max.

    delight   delighted   delightful

2. The bride's and groom's _____ was obvious to everyone at the wedding.

    happy   happier   happiness

3. Can you bring me a _____ of grapes?

    hand   handy   handful

4. The sky got _____ as the storm came closer.

    black   blacker   blackness

5. I didn't know your brother was such a _____ person.

    helper   helpful   helped

6. Which _____ has on the uniform with number 1?

    play   playful   player

7. There is always a _____ supply of fruit in Jean's refrigerator.

    plenty   plentiful   plant

8. Everyone loves Mrs. Scott because she is so _____.

    kindness   kind   kinder

9. We were speechless at the _____ of the mountains.

    awful   awesomeness   awesome

10. A trip to the moon used to be a _____ idea.

    fanciful   fancy   fancied

11. Rosa's grandfather is a _____ politician.

    powerful   power   powered

12. _____ is not one of Carl's major traits.

    Polite   Politeness   Politely

Directions: Read the following letter. Circle each word that contains a suffix you have studied in this unit. You should circle 21 words in all. Then write each word you have circled on one of the lines at the bottom. The suffixes you have studied are listed.

er	or	ist	est	ee	eer	ent	ant	ward	en
		ize	ful	ness					

Dearest Grandma,

I must apologize for not writing sooner. We had a dreadful prairie storm many weeks ago, and I still get nervous whenever the wind begins to blow. The awesomeness of nature is overwhelming sometimes. And the wildness of this new land is so different from our civilized city home back there with you.

We had a visitor last week. A doctor traveling westward spent several days with us. He is a specialist in troubles of the bones and gave Papa some excellent advice for his arthritis. Papa says he was far better than the one back home, whom he says is really only a profiteer.

Mama is busier every day with her orchard. The apples should start to ripen any day. I act as her assistant, but I'm afraid I have much to learn before I become a farmer.

Please do not worry about us. You must realize that it is fun to be a resident of a new land. And if we do not like it here, we can always move onward.

Love,

Charlotte

1. _____   7. _____   13. _____   19. _____

2. _____   8. _____   14. _____   20. _____

3. _____   9. _____   15. _____   21. _____

4. _____   10. _____   16. _____

5. _____   11. _____   17. _____

6. _____   12. _____   18. _____

Directions: Read the following short paragraphs, then answer the questions below.

A. Buy the "Wrestler Body Building Kit." It will strengthen your body and make you stronger than anyone else. Move forward with "Wrestler."

B. Dear Editor:

Our city is the best because we have the best mayor. We are very proud that he is a nominee for governor. He is intelligent, cheerful, and helpful. Also, he is interested in our schools.

We do not look forward to losing such a good leader, but we hope our citizens will vote for Sam Brown for governor.

Sincerely yours,
Fifth Grade—Oak Valley School

C. Dear Sonia,

We are hopeful that you will be our visitor over the holidays. There will be a guitarist in town whom I think you would enjoy. And the art museum has an exhibit by your favorite painter. It is our busiest time at the store, but we will always make time for our delightful granddaughter.

Love,
Grandpa

1. What does Paragraph A try to persuade someone to do?

_____

_____

2. What does Paragraph B try to persuade someone to do?

_____

_____

3. What does Paragraph C try to persuade someone to do?

_____

_____

Directions: Write a word from the paragraphs that has one of the following suffixes.

or	ward	ful

1. _____ 2. _____ 3. _____

● The suffixes **hood, ship,** and **ment** usually mean **the state or condition of being.**

word	definition
childhood	the state or condition of being a child
leadership	the state or condition of being a leader
retirement	the state or condition of being retired

Directions: Read the following paragraph. Circle each word that has the suffix **hood, ship,** or **ment.**

Our neighborhood track team won the championship this fall. There was a lot of excitement over this accomplishment. The township has even talked about the likelihood of buying trophies for the members of the team. The leadership of Mari Evans is one factor in the team's improvement this season. There is surely no argument about that.

Directions: Now write the correct circled word on the line next to its definition.

1. something done well _____

2. place where people live _____ or _____

3. probability _____

4. something that has gotten better _____

5. quarrel _____

6. first place position _____

7. great thrill _____

8. guidance, direction _____

TRACK CHAMPS

Directions: Read the list of roots below. Then read the incomplete sentences. Make a new word using a root and the suffix **hood, ship,** or **ment.** Write the new word on the line.

retire   false   equip
settle   author   relation
pay   child   improve
governor

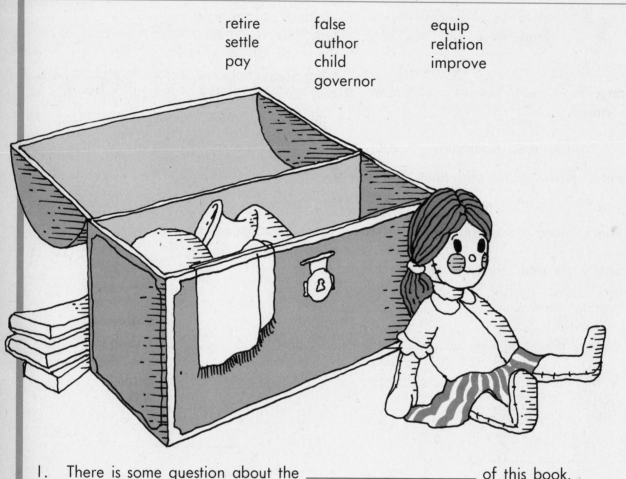

1.   There is some question about the _____ of this book.

2.   What will your grandfather do after his _____?

3.   The doctor did not notice any _____ in the accident patient.

4.   In the old trunk I found a doll my grandma had played with during her

     _____.

5.   There is no _____ between the artist and the child she painted.

6.   The lawyers tried to talk their clients into agreeing to a _____.

7.   This car repair _____ can be stored in the garage.

8.   When is the first _____ due on Mom's new car?

9.   A newspaper editor must be careful not to print a _____.

10. Maria Oates is seeking the _____ of our state.

● The suffixes **able** and **ible** usually mean **able to be** or **full of.**

word	definition
washable	able to be washed
sensible	full of sense

Directions: Choose the correct word from the list to complete each sentence, and write it on the line. Notice that when the root ends in **e** or **y**, these letters are dropped before the suffix is added.

reliable	breakable	eatable
profitable	washable	reducible
reversible	readable	defensible
	collapsible	

1. When clothing can be cleaned at home, we say it is _____.

2. When something can be made smaller, we say it is _____.

3. When some activity makes a lot of money, we say it is _____.

4. When something can be damaged if it is dropped,

   we say it is _____.

5. When a jacket can be worn on both sides, we say it is _____.

6. When food is not spoiled, we say it is _____.

7. When something can be read, we say it is _____.

8. When something can be defended, we say it is _____.

9. When something can be relied on, we say

   it is _____.

10. When something can be taken apart and put in a

    smaller package, we say it is _____.

Directions: Read each sentence. Underline each word containing the suffix **able** or **ible**. Then write the root of each underlined word on the line next to the sentence.

1. Tanya is an adorable child. _____

2. She is quite sensible, too. _____

3. Alex gets into some laughable situations. _____

4. Sometimes his actions are unpredictable. _____

5. We tried every conceivable solution to the puzzle. _____

6. My little brother was responsible for solving the mystery when no one else could.

    _____

7. My hamster is a lovable animal. _____

8. However, my dog is also likable. _____

9. I like riding in Joe's convertible. _____

10. It's really a comfortable car. _____

11. That wasn't a very charitable remark you made about Ann's drawing.

    _____

12. You're right, I will try to be more favorable. _____

13. Micki's contraption was usable for predicting tomorrow's weather.

    _____

● The suffixes **ion, ation,** and **ition** usually mean **the act of** or **the condition of being.**

word	definition
presentation	the act of presenting
exhaustion	the condition of being exhausted

Directions: Choose the word that best completes each sentence, and write it on the line.

1. What is your _____ to our going jogging?
   object/objection

2. Will you help me _____ this story?
   illustrate/illustration

3. The two main problems for long distance swimmers are cold and

   _____.
   exhaust/exhaustion

4. By my _____ the answer to the math problem is 242.
   calculate/calculation

5. Did you _____ two seats at the restaurant for dinner?
   reserve/reservation

6. Bridget can _____ the voice of every member of her family.
   imitate/imitation

7. Homer and Corrie went to the _____ for world peace.
   demonstrate/demonstration

8. Will you _____ a song for my birthday?
   compose/composition

9. My brother made an _____ against me when he couldn't find his
   accuse/accusation
   baseball glove.

10. The world's _____ is growing faster each year.
    populate/population

11. My sister is going to try to _____ a baby.
    adopt/adoption

12. Will Maria have to learn to take _____ for her new job?
    dictate/dictation

● When a word ends in **e** or **y,** drop the **e** or suffix with **y** before adding **ion, ation,** or **ition.**

Directions: Add the suffix **ion** to each word below. Write the new word on the line.

1. invent _____

2. secrete _____

3. exhibit _____

4. celebrate _____

5. inspect _____

6. persecute _____

Directions: Choose the correct word from the ones you made above to complete each sentence below.

1. Have you seen the new _____ of animal photographs at the museum?

2. Your high grades deserve a _____.

3. Wasps hold their nests together with the use of a _____ from their bodies.

4. Did your newly cleaned room pass Dad's _____?

Directions: Add the suffix **ation** to each word below. Write the new word on the line. Remember the rule above.

1. imagine _____

2. quote _____

3. public _____

4. confirm _____

5. capitalize _____

6. civilize _____

Directions: Choose the correct word from the ones you made above to complete each sentence below.

1. I'm going to use a _____ by Dr. Martin Luther King in my speech.

2. Did the airline give you a _____ on your tickets?

3. Sal has the wildest _____ of anyone I know.

4. The archaeologists discovered the ruins of an acient _____.

● The suffixes **ance, ence,** and **ity** usually mean **quality** or **fact of being.** The suffix **ive** usually means **likely to** or **having to do with.**

word	definition
importance	the quality or state of being important
reality	the quality or state of being real
impressive	likely to impress
massive	having to do with size, mass, or weight

Directions: Read each sentence below. Then answer the question by writing the correct word on the line.

1. The avalanche sent a heavy amount of snow down the mountain and into the village.

   What is another word for **heavy?** _____

   active   massive   disruptive

2. The salesperson has great honesty, and I trust her.

   What is another word for **honesty?** _____

   sincerity   personality   popularity

3. The displays in that store window have a lot of novelty.

   What is another word for **novelty?** _____
   originality   publicity   maturity

4. I sometimes confuse the identical twins because there is so much similarity between them.

   What is another word for **similarity?** _____
   acceptance   observance   resemblance

5. My grandpa has a firm belief in healthful exercise.
   What is another word for **belief?**

   _____

   competence   confidence   coincidence

6. Those colored lights are very pretty and ornamental.
   What is another word for **ornamental?**

   _____

   effective   disruptive   decorative

7. Regina is an energetic basketball player.
   What is another word for **energetic?**

   _____

   adhesive   alternative   aggressive

● An **analogy** tells the relationship that one thing has to another thing.

These are examples of analogies: **Car** is to **garage** as **airplane** is to **hangar**.
Kitten is to **cat** as **puppy** is to **dog**.
Huge is to **massive** as **honesty** is to **sincerity**.

Directions: Circle the correct ending for each analogy below. Use your dictionary if you need to.

1. **Dynamite** is to **explosive** as **tape** is to _____.

   adhesive   impressive   selective

2. **Helping** is to **assistance** as **watching** is to _____.

   hindrance   observance   coincidence

3. **Negative** is to **positive** as **criminality** is to _____.

   simplicity   complexity   legality

4. **Dance** is to **activity** as **uproar** is to _____.

   disturbance   attendance   guidance

5. **King** is to **nobility** as **person** is to _____.

   maturity   publicity   humanity

6. **Leading** is to **guidance** as **forgiving** is to _____.

   insurance   tolerance   observance

7. **Offensive** is to **defensive** as **superiority** is to _____.

   security   inferiority   popularity

8. **Unusual** is to **distinctive** as **pretty** is to _____.

   attractive   selective   executive

9. **Advertisement** is to **publicity** as **generator** is to _____.

   mortality   electricity   legality

Directions: Read the letter below. Draw a line under each word that contains one of the suffixes in the list. Then circle the suffix. You will underline fifteen words.

SUFFIXES

hood	ion	ance	ive
ship	ation	ence	able
ment	ition	ity	ible

Dear Molly,

    We want you to visit us soon. We are getting ready for a big celebration on the Fourth of July in honor of Independence Day. The whole neighborhood is involved in the preparation. Each street is responsible for one float. There will be a prize for the float that shows the most creativity and imagination. Some look quite impressive already. It is conceivable that ours will receive some recognition.

    The parade will begin at noon. There will be police clearance all along the parade route to Settlement Park. There will be games and plenty of refreshments available at the park.

    I hope you can join us to have some fun and to renew our friendship.

Yours truly,

Diana

● The topics below all are examples of persuasion. **Persuasion** is trying to convince someone to do something or think a certain way.

Directions: Put a check mark in front of the topic that you would like to write about.

_____ convincing someone to give up eating junk food

_____ convincing a classmate to study harder

_____ persuading someone to buy Girl Scout cookies

_____ making up an advertisement telling why a certain product is good for dogs or cats

_____ convincing a friend to participate in a sport

_____ _____

(my idea)

Directions: Do some persuasive writing about the topic you picked. Clearly state what your opinion is about the topic. Then tell why you have that opinion. Use at least three words that contain a suffix that you have learned about in this unit.

_____

_____

_____

_____

_____

_____

_____

_____

_____

_____

Directions: Now go back and proofread your writing. Circle each word that contains a suffix that you have learned about in this unit.

● When a short-vowel word ends in a single consonant, usually double the consonant before adding a suffix that begins with a vowel.

Directions: Circle each root that ends in a single consonant. Then form new words by putting each root and suffix together. Write the new words on the lines.

rub + ing _____	strut + ed _____
laugh + ing _____	hit + er _____
jog + ing _____	fat + est _____
quick + est _____	plan + ing _____
rob + er _____	stun + ed _____
chap + ed _____	fast + er _____
start + ing _____	skid + ed _____
hot + er _____	shut + er _____
grin + ing _____	refresh + ed _____
shrug + ing _____	throb + ing _____

Directions: Draw a circle around each word that doubles the final consonant to add a suffix. Then write its root on the line.

1. Jim grabbed the ball and hurled it to second base. _____

2. The sailor knotted the rope on the mast. _____

3. Sheila is swapping her turtle for a lizard. _____

4. The nervous outfielder dropped the ball. _____

5. The mouse we chose was the fattest in the cage. _____

6. Holiday shoppers sometimes crowd the sidewalks. _____

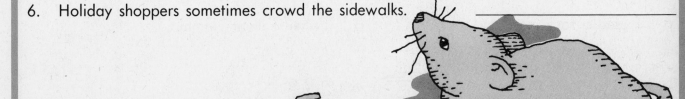

Directions: Circle each suffix below that begins with a vowel. Then form new words by putting each root and suffix together. Write the new words on the lines.

scan + ing _____   bask + ing _____

hot + est _____   sad + ness _____

steep + er _____   plot + ed _____

entertain + ment _____   hard + ness _____

drip + ed _____   snap + ing _____

heart + less _____   wet + est _____

cram + ed _____   cheer + ful _____

rapid + ly _____   strap + ed _____

Directions: Circle the root in each word in the list. Then complete each sentence with a word from the list.

throbbing	pitting	eagerly
shredded	openly	flippers
squatted	hitter	equipment
trapper	readable	dimmest
quitter	popping	wrapping

1. A ladder and hose are fire-fighting _____.

2. Jane _____ cheese to sprinkle over the casserole.

3. The cook is _____ the cherries before he bakes the pie.

4. When Vicki walked into the room I was _____ her birthday present.

5. He _____ down to help his little sister tie her shoes.

6. I used a face mask and _____ when I went swimming.

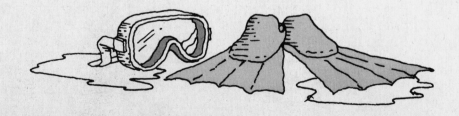

● When a word ends in final **e,** drop the **e** before adding a suffix that begins with a vowel.

Directions: Form new words by adding the suffixes **es, ed,** and **ing.**

	es	ed	ing
squeeze	_____	_____	_____
disapprove	_____	_____	_____
bribe	_____	_____	_____
hope	_____	_____	_____
imagine	_____	_____	_____

Directions: Form new words by adding the suffixes **er** and **est.**

	er	est
late	_____	_____
little	_____	_____
humble	_____	_____
nice	_____	_____
strange	_____	_____

Directions: Write the root for each of the following words.

cradles	_____	approved	_____
observer	_____	pavement	_____
latest	_____	grazing	_____
sprinkler	_____	changed	_____
scraping	_____	safest	_____
decided	_____	combining	_____
trader	_____	scrambled	_____

127

● When a word ends in final **e,** drop the **e** before adding a suffix that begins with a vowel.

Directions: Add the suffix to the root below the line to complete each sentence. Use your dictionary for the correct spelling if you need to.

1. Even _____ rain at the picnic couldn't dampen everyone's good
   drizzle + ing
   time.

2. The _____ for <u>United States</u> is U.S.
   abbreviate + ion

3. The students play hopscotch on the schoolyard _____.
   pave + ment

4. The storekeeper greeted the customers with _____.
   polite + ness

5. Donna _____ pepper over her baked potato.
   sprinkle + ed

6. From now on, Tom has _____ to be on time.
   promise + ed

7. We had the best time _____ at the carnival.
   imagine + able

8. The teacher cut an apple into two parts as a _____ of what one-
   demonstrate + ion
   half means.

9. Throwing away good food is _____.
   waste + ful

10. It's _____ to drive slowly on icy roads.
    advise + able

11. The _____ boy lost his watch.
    care + less

12. The _____ from outer space wanted to help earthlings.
    strange + ers

128

Directions: Many words have more than one suffix. Read each word in the list below. Underline the first suffix and circle the second suffix. Remember, **s** can be a suffix.

watchfully	operations	painlessly	trumpeters	skillfully
carelessness	widening	publications	frightfulness	descendants
enlightening	attractions	thoughtfulness	powerlessness	celebrations
moistened	cheerfulness	joyfully	hopefully	attendances

Directions: Circle the word in each sentence with more than one suffix. Then write its root on the line.

1. The court is legalizing bicycle licenses. _____

2. We were saddened to hear that you lost your pet. _____

3. Betty thought that running in the rain puddles for fun was foolishness. _____

4. The day was wonderfully sunny and warm. _____

5. Hopefully, the final test will not be difficult. _____

6. The pencils whose points are broken need to be sharpened. _____

7. Migrations of many birds occur in the fall. _____

8. A tornado touched down and completely flattened the barn. _____

Directions: In each sentence, circle the two words with more than one suffix. Then write each root on the line. Remember, **s** can be a suffix.

1. The inventiveness of the engineers was awarded when they won the prize.

   _____   _____

2. The cheerfulness of the host and hostess lightened everyone's hearts.

   _____   _____

3. A surgeon performs all operations with carefulness.

   _____   _____

4. The peacefulness of the sleeping puppy softened her heart.

   _____   _____

5. The spectators' shouts rose, and the racer's heartbeat quickened.

   _____   _____

6. Teddy accepts corrections surprisingly well.

   _____   _____

7. The loud party awakened everyone in the nearby neighborhoods.

   _____   _____

8. As she thought longingly of her homeland, raindrops moistened her face.

   _____   _____

9. The acceptances to the party invitations came in the mail.

   _____   _____

10. The vacationer found the new campers' areas clean.

    _____   _____

11. Everyone felt heartened at the hopefulness in the football captain's speech.

    _____   _____

● If a word ends in **y** preceded by a consonant, change the **y** to **i** and add **es** to make the word plural. If a word ends in **y** preceded by a vowel, just add **s** to make the word plural.

activity—activities   chimney—chimneys

Directions: Write the plural form of each word.

story _____   army _____   holiday _____

canary _____   donkey _____   missionary _____

company _____   injury _____   valley _____

decoy _____   victory _____   library _____

country _____   bay _____   mystery _____

● If a word ends in **y** preceded by a consonant, change the **y** to **i** when any suffix is added except **ing.** If a word ends in **y** preceded by a vowel, just add the suffix.

heavy—heavier   study—studying   delay—delayed

Directions: Write the root ending in y of each word below.

peppiest _____   dustier _____

mutinied _____   keyed _____

worrying _____   tardiest _____

rustier _____   flies _____

obeys _____   luckiest _____

fancier _____   multiplying _____

relayed _____   carried _____

Directions: Form a new word by putting each root and suffix together. Write the new word on the line. Remember the rules for adding suffixes to words.

lucky + er _____   greasy + est _____

worry + ed _____   easy + er _____

obey + s _____   occupy + ed _____

sleepy + est _____   bossy + er _____

salty + er _____   toy + ed _____

fancy + est _____   heavy + er _____

Directions: Use the words you formed to complete the sentences. The correct answers will give you the answer to the riddle. The directions below will tell you what to do with the circled letters.

Riddle: What is the best material for kites?

1. Cinderella had the ⊖ _ _ _ _ _ _ _ gown at the ball.

2. A person who wins at bingo is ⊖ _ _ _ _ _ _ than people who lose.

3. The typewriter broke down after the child _ _ _ ⊖ _ _ with it.

4. Rip Van Winkle, who slept for 20 years, is perhaps the _ _ _ _ ⊖ _ _ _ _ character in any book.

5. Popcorn and potato chips are often _ ⊖ _ _ _ _ _ than other foods.

6. The Jones family _ _ _ _ ⊖ _ _ _ the apartment on the first floor until they moved.

7. The opposite of <u>harder</u> is _ _ _ _ ⊖ _.

8. A piano is much _ _ _ _ _ _ ⊖ to carry than a violin.

Directions: Now write each circled letter from the answers in order, and you will find out the answer to the riddle.

Riddle answer: _ _ _ _ _ _ _ _

● If a word ends in **y** preceded by a consonant, change the **y** to **i** when adding the suffix **ly.**

heavy + ly—heavily

There are a few exceptions such as **dryly, shyly,** and **slyly.**

● If a word ends in **y** preceded by a vowel, just add the suffix **ly.**

coy + ly—coyly

● When **ly** is added to a word ending in **le,** the le is dropped. Otherwise the word would be difficult to pronounce.

wobble + ly—wobbly

Directions: Add **ly** to each word. Write the new word on the line.

noisy	_____	busy	_____	drizzle	_____
greedy	_____	bubble	_____	dizzy	_____
hasty	_____	giggle	_____	merry	_____
pebble	_____	probable	_____	lucky	_____

Directions: Write the root for each underlined word.

1. The knight <u>nobly</u> risked his life to save the king. _____

2. Connie yawned <u>sleepily</u> as she turned off the TV. _____

3. The monkey scampered <u>nimbly</u> from limb to limb. _____

4. The <u>wiggly</u> arms of the squid entertained the people watching it at the aquarium. _____

5. Jane <u>easily</u> passed the test for her driver's license. _____

6. Brightly colored curtains <u>prettily</u> decorated the kitchen. _____

7. Jan hobbled <u>feebly</u> down the hospital hall. _____

8. "Have a good day!" said the storekeeper <u>cheerily</u>. _____

Directions: Complete each sentence by adding **ly** to each root under the line. Write the new word on the line.

1. The librarian asked the _____ children to be quiet.

giggle

2. Lori _____ had an extra set of keys when her first set was locked

lucky

inside the car.

3. Small waves _____ lapped the shore.

lazy

4. The cactus certainly is _____.

prickle

5. Tim dresses _____ when he washes and waxes the car.

sloppy

6. It was difficult to walk barefooted on the _____ beach.

pebble

7. The nurse _____ bandaged the child's cut.

reliable

8. The movie ended _____ for the hero and heroine.

happy

9. I wouldn't sit on that _____ chair if I were you.

wobble

10. The chipmunks left _____ when they heard footsteps approaching

hasty

the tree.

11. It was fun to watch the _____ worms on my worm farm.

wiggle

12. Eating _____ every day helps keep an athlete fit.

healthy

13. We needed umbrellas to protect us from the _____ weather.

drizzle

14. The crowd _____ clamored for a new pitcher to be sent in.

noisy

15. The students _____ skipped home on the last day of school.

merry

134

Directions: Add the suffixes to the roots to form new words. Complete each story on this page and page 136 by writing the new words on the lines.

Throughout history, the _____ of people has _____
(invent + ive + ness)   (produce + ed)

many _____ _____. _____ have
(amaze + ing)   (accomplish + ments)   (Invent + or + s)

used their _____ and _____ to benefit all human
(imagine + ation + s)   (skill + ful + ness)

beings. Consider Levi Hutchins, a clockmaker, who _____ during the
(live + ed)

1700s. He worked very _____ every day and seldom
(busy + ly)

_____ any time. Levi _____ to rise at 4 a.m. each
(waste + ed)   (try + ed)

day—no _____ for him! Not _____, he
(lazy + ness)   (surprise + ing + ly)

sometimes overslept. This greatly _____ Levi. One day, the idea of
(annoy + ed)

_____ an alarm clock struck Levi. His _____
(make + ing)   (invent + ion)

worked _____ and _____. Ever after, Levi was
(simple + ly)   (success + ful + ly)

_____ at 4 a.m. He never _____ for a patent.
(awake + en + ed)   (apply + ed)

Money was _____ unimportant to him. All he wanted was a
(seem + ing + ly)

_____ way of _____ up on time.
(depend + able)   (wake + ing)

Harvey Kennedy, on the other hand, _____ benefited from his
(profit + able + ly)

_____. He invented the shoelace, and made two and one-half million
(ability + es)

Go on to next page.

dollars on it. People bought it _____ because they were

immediate + ly

_____ of _____ , _____ , and

tire + ed   pin + ing   strap + ing

_____ their shoes.

buckle + ing

Directions: Write **T** if the statement is **true.** Write **F** if it is **false.** Look back at the story on page 135 if you need to.

1. _____ Inventors' abilities help others.
2. _____ Levi Hutchins avoided hard work.
3. _____ Levi hated to oversleep.
4. _____ Levi made an alarm clock that worked.
5. _____ Levi made lots of money on his invention.
6. _____ Harvey Kennedy never applied for a patent.
7. _____ Harvey Kennedy invented the shoelace.
8. _____ Before the shoelace, people had to pin, strap, or buckle their shoes.
9. _____ It took a long time for Harvey's invention to catch on.

Outlines help you summarize an article for study, or to prepare a speech. An outline may be written in question-and-answer form. Complete the outline below for the stories of the two inventors. The outline will present the main facts. One answer is filled in for you. You can fill in the rest of the answers to finish the outline.

Title   Two Unique Inventors

First
Heading   I. Levi Hutchins

      A. What invented? *alarm clock* _____

      B. Why? _____

      C. How did he benefit? _____

      _____

Second
Heading   II. Harvey Kennedy

      A. What invented? _____

      B. Why did people like it? _____

      _____

      C. How much did he make? _____

● If a word ends in **f** or **fe,** the **f** or **fe** is usually changed to **v** and **es** is added to make the word plural. **Chief, belief, reef,** and **roof** are four exceptions. Any word that ends in double **f (ff)** is made plural by adding **s.**

Directions: Complete each sentence by writing the plural form of each underlined word on the line.

1. One <u>calf</u> is grazing. All the other _____ are in the barn.

2. The wolf gave a big <u>huff</u>. But all his _____ couldn't blow the brick house down.

3. The child wore one <u>scarf</u> on his head and two _____ around his neck.

4. One <u>loaf</u> of bread is eaten. There are two other _____ in the breadbox.

5. Since Betty is afraid of _____, she ran for the cabin when she heard a <u>wolf</u> howl.

6. That <u>cliff</u> is the steepest of all the _____ that Teddy has climbed.

7. Only one <u>leaf</u> lay on the grass after Liz raked the _____.

8. The horse's hind left <u>hoof</u> was sore, but the other _____ were fine.

9. "We need new carving _____," said Jane. "I can't find one good <u>knife</u> in the house."

10. The <u>chief</u> of the Hopi Indians spoke to the other _____ about peace.

11. The wind blew one <u>sheaf</u> of the teacher's papers across the road. Luckily the other

    _____ were caught in time.

12. The police caught one <u>thief</u> but the other

    two _____ are still at large.

Directions: Write the plural form of each word.

belief _____   calf _____   dwarf _____

half _____   knife _____   whiff _____

cuff _____   wife _____   chief _____

life _____   staff _____   loaf _____

scarf _____   shelf _____   thief _____

Directions: Use the plural words you wrote to answer the questions below.

1. Who are leaders of tribes? _____

2. Which are kitchen tools used to cut and slice? _____

3. What are the shapes that breads come in? _____

4. On what can you place books? _____

5. Which two of these make one whole? _____

6. What does a cat supposedly have nine of? _____

7. What do you call young cattle? _____

8. What do you call ideas you think are true or real? _____

9. Who are the partners of husbands? _____

10. What can people wear on their head and tie under their chin? _____

138

● If a word ends in **o,** just **s** is usually added to make the word plural. Some exceptions are made plural by adding **es.**

potato—potatoes   **tomato—tomatoes**   **hero—heroes**

Directions: Complete each sentence by writing the plural form of the word at the right.

1. _____ are violent wind storms.   Tornado

2. Some people like to wear _____ instead of coats.   poncho

3. _____ are a food that can be cooked in many different   Potato
ways.

4. Terraces made of flat stones for outdoor eating are called

_____.   patio

5. _____ are a good source of vitamin C.   Tomato

6. People who are admired for great deeds may be called

_____.   hero

7. You can make a wonderful snack dip by adding a little lemon juice and

mayonnaise to _____.   avocado

8. _____ are small, shrill-sounding flutes.   Piccolo

9. _____ are like violins, but are very much larger and have   Cello
lower tones.

10. At _____ cowboys and cowgirls compete at roping cattle
and riding bucking broncos.   rodeo

11. _____ are huts that Eskimos build using frozen blocks of   Igloo
snow.

12. Female _____ carry their young around with them.   kangaroo

139

Directions: Write the plural form of each word.

piano _____	alto _____	photo _____
igloo _____	piccolo _____	tornado _____
poncho_____	avocado _____	tomato _____
hero _____	banjo _____	cello _____
patio _____	rodeo _____	potato _____
solo _____	sombrero_____	kangaroo_____

Directions: Use the plural words you wrote to answer the questions below.

1. Which words name musical instruments?

   _____ _____ _____ _____

2. What are cowboy and cowgirl contests called? _____

3. Which kind of vegetable tastes good in all these forms: mashed, french-fried, baked,

   and scalloped? _____

4. What are terrible wind storms called? _____

5. What are people called who do brave and wonderful deeds? _____

6. Which vegetables are used to make spaghetti sauce and ketchup?

   _____

7. What are pictures that have been taken with a camera called? _____

8. What are large waterproof cloaks often worn by campers? _____

9. What are dome-shaped huts made of snow? _____

10. What are outdoor courtyards? _____

11. What musical instruments have eighty-eight keys? _____

● Some words do not change at all in their plural form.

Directions: The words in the exercise below are the same in their singular and plural forms. If the word names a food that comes from a plant, write **P.** If it names an animal or food that comes from an animal, write **A.**

_____ spinach	_____ moose	_____ cattle
_____ deer	_____ rye	_____ butter
_____ fish	_____ milk	_____ sheep
_____ broccoli	_____ popcorn	_____ bacon
_____ sauerkraut	_____ oatmeal	_____ salmon
_____ spaghetti	_____ trout	_____ honey
_____ cod	_____ zucchini	_____ shrimp
_____ haddock	_____ bread	_____ wheat

● Some words change completely in their plural form.

Directions: Write the missing letters to make the plural form of the words below.

foot – f_____t	man – m_____n
child – child_____	woman – wom_____n
goose – g_____se	mouse – m_____
ox – ox_____	tooth – t_____th

● Some other plural forms may not be familiar to you. Try to memorize them.

Directions: Write the correct plural form next to each meaning.

singular	plural
cactus	cacti
fungus	fungi
crisis	crises

1. _____ times of danger or anxious waiting

2. _____ desert plants that usually have sharp spines and no leaves

3. _____ plants such as mushrooms, toadstools, and molds

Directions: Use the words in the list to work through the crossword puzzle.

sauerkraut	cacti	mice	sheep	cattle	deer
bacon	popcorn	geese	salmon	women	teeth
oatmeal	wheat	moose	men	spaghetti	crises

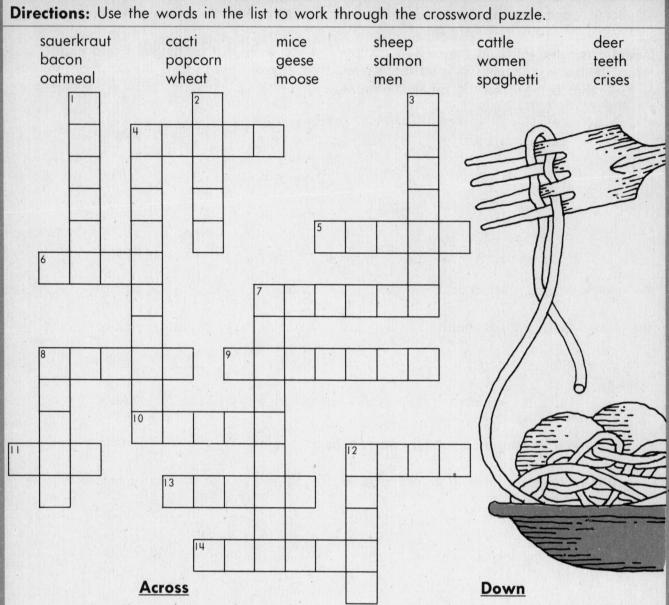

Across

4. farm animals sheared for their wool
5. salted, smoked meat often served with eggs
6. swift animals living in the woods
7. large ocean fish that swim up rivers to lay their eggs
8. cereal grasses used for making flour
9. cooked cereal made from ground, boiled oats
10. what you use to bite and chew food
11. more than one male
12. small rodents found in houses and fields
13. prickly plants you wouldn't want to sit on
14. stressful, anxious times

Down

1. animals of the cow family
2. large birds that honk and fly in V formations to migrate
3. corn that turns into white puffs when heated
4. cabbage that's spiced and tastes sour
7. Italian dish made with pasta and tomato sauce
8. more than one female
12. large woodland animals with wide antlers

142

Remember these rules:

- Double vowels stand for only one vowel sound. (inst<u>ea</u>d, sp<u>oo</u>nful)

- A prefix or suffix is a syllable in itself if it contains a vowel sound. (<u>pre</u>wash, old<u>en</u>)

- Some prefixes and suffixes have more than one syllable (<u>ultra</u>fine, <u>super</u>human)

Directions: Read each word. Then write the number of vowels you see and the number of vowel sounds you hear, and the number of syllables in each word.

	Vowels Seen	Vowel Sounds	Syllables		Vowels Seen	Vowel Sounds	Syllables
congratulations	____	____	____	insight	____	____	____
encountered	____	____	____	exclamation	____	____	____
exaggerating	____	____	____	kangaroos	____	____	____
irresponsible	____	____	____	excitably	____	____	____
determination	____	____	____	handkerchiefs	____	____	____
indirectly	____	____	____	irritability	____	____	____
invisible	____	____	____	resolution	____	____	____
foreshadows	____	____	____	pavement	____	____	____
imprisoned	____	____	____	organizations	____	____	____
illogical	____	____	____	squeezing	____	____	____
torpedoes	____	____	____	scrubber	____	____	____
motionless	____	____	____	noisiest	____	____	____
quickened	____	____	____	sleepily	____	____	____
observer	____	____	____	entrusting	____	____	____
combinations	____	____	____	feebly	____	____	____

Directions: See if you can find the fourteen plural forms of words in the puzzle below. Work from left to right and then from top to bottom. The words can appear horizontally or vertically. Circle the words as you find them. Write them on the lines. Then divide them into syllables using vertical lines.

```
P  C  F  C  A  C  T  I  N  X  Y  Z
O  A  T  M  E  A  L  J  M  N  P  R
P  W  C  S  W  V  E  H  O  N  E  Y
C  E  D  P  A  I  R  L  A  U  P  E
O  C  E  A  B  C  H  E  R  O  E  S
R  L  F  G  P  I  C  C  O  L  O  S
N  M  H  H  M  I  Y  D  A  W  A  C
G  R  D  E  E  R  A  P  U  O  V  E
L  G  K  T  E  E  T  O  C  M  E  F
C  O  R  T  O  M  A  T  O  E  S  G
C  P  A  I  D  Z  O  A  L  N  E  S
M  A  P  B  C  A  T  T  L  E  O  R
S  H  R  I  M  P  E  O  B  T  K  L
G  U  O  Z  O  B  E  E  S  R  S  T
M  Z  T  O  A  E  L  S  B  M  N  O
```

_____   _____

_____   _____

_____   _____

_____   _____

_____   _____

Remember:

● Divide a compound word between the words that make the compound word.

ear/drum   hand/bag   spell/down

Directions: Underline the compound words in the sentences. Then divide them into syllables by drawing vertical lines.

1.   The nighttime watchman works until dawn.

2.   They had a feast eating chicken drumsticks and cornbread.

3.   We must help safeguard the wildlife in national parks.

4.   Smokestacks were puffing and fires blazing during the heavy snowfall.

5.   The plan to surprise the teacher on her birthday went as smoothly as clockwork.

6.   Students in the classroom were unwrapping new phonics workbooks.

● When a word ends in **le** preceded by a consonant, divide the word before that consonant.

Directions: Divide these words into syllables using vertical lines.

cradle	angle	bottle	paddle	puzzle
ample	grumble	crumble	noble	gentle
handle	poodle	baffle	purple	mumble
fiddle	cripple	jungle	people	wobble
battle	dimple	fumble	startle	bridle

145

● A word has as many syllables as it has vowel sounds. Some prefixes and suffixes can have more than one syllable.

Directions: On the first line after each word, write the number of syllables in the word. On the second line, divide the word into syllables using vertical lines.

protest	_____	_____	hunger	_____	_____
wondering	_____	_____	taxation	_____	_____
famous	_____	_____	recess	_____	_____
watermelon	_____	_____	sudden	_____	_____
insects	_____	_____	whistle	_____	_____
sofa	_____	_____	poodle	_____	_____
strawberries	_____	_____	giggled	_____	_____

startle   _____ _____

wiggle   _____ _____

skyscraper   _____ _____

tablespoon   _____ _____

prisons   _____ _____

wintertime   _____ _____

windowpane   _____ _____

shopkeeper   _____ _____

shipmate   _____ _____

stepladder   _____ _____

enjoyed   _____ _____

wagons   _____ _____

Directions: Read the article. Complete each unfinished sentence by writing the plural form of each word on the line above it.

There were many famous Indian _____ in North America. Among
                                          chief

the most famous is a Cherokee brave named Sequoyah. He had noticed white

_____ and _____ reading. He called their papers
         man   woman

"talking _____." Members of his tribe held the _____
              leaf   belief

that reading was a gift of the Great Spirit and that it was not a human discovery.

Sequoyah disagreed. "You _____ could read if there was a way to write
                              yourself

our language," he said. For years, Sequoyah worked at figuring out signs for the sounds

he heard. He wrote them with _____ in bark, or with sticks on dirt. He
                                       knife

received only _____ from his tribe. His own wife, like all other
                     rebuff

_____ in the tribe, thought he was foolish. Yet, Sequoyah enriched the
         wife

_____ of the Cherokee Indians. After 12 years, he had invented a simple
         life

Cherokee alphabet. Within a few days, almost all _____,
                                                         man

_____, and _____ in the tribe could read!
         woman   child

Sequoyah became one of the great _____ of the Cherokee nation.
                                          hero

There are no _____ of Sequoyah, but a painting of him survives today.
                     photo

● An **outline** helps you summarize the important ideas in a story or article. A **topic outline** is written with simple words or short phrases.

Directions: Read the story. Then circle the answer to each question.

The Indians of the High Plains were always on the move. They set up no permanent villages because they needed to keep on the move in search of buffaloes. Their homes were portable tepees—poles covered with hides. The arrival of the wild horse on the plains made life much easier for the Plains hunters. Braves became some of the best horseback riders in the world.

The Plains Indians had several uses for the buffaloes they hunted. They used the hides to cover their homes. The fur was used for blankets. They ate the animals' meat. Even the horns were used. Jewelry and tools were carved from them.

1. What is the article about?   Plains Indians   Cherokees   Buffaloes

2. What is the first paragraph about?   . Types of homes   How they worshipped

3. What is the second paragraph about?   Uses of the buffaloes   Hunting the buffaloes

4. Why were their lives unsettled?

     Moved searching buffaloes   Moved finding farmland

5. What kinds of shelter did they have?   Tepee homes   Long houses

6. What did the Plains Indians become?   Good farmers   Excellent horseback riders

Directions: Now use the answers you circled to complete the outline below.

Title   _____
                    (Answer to Question 1)

First   I. _____
Heading   (Answer to Question 2)

          A. _____
               (Answer to Question 4)

          B. _____
               (Answer to Question 5)

          C. _____
               (Answer to Question 6)

● Words are arranged in alphabetical order in a dictionary. When words begin with the same letter or letters, look at the second or next letter to put the words in alphabetical order.

Directions: Number the words in each column to show the alphabetical order. Remember to look at the second letter of each word.

1. payment _____	2. swaying _____	3. awkward _____
position _____	strawberry _____	arrive _____
planter _____	seashore _____	amount _____
pension _____	skateboard _____	application _____
prance _____	sickness _____	aching _____

Directions: Now number the words in these columns to show the alphabetical order. Look at the third letter of each word.

1. crayon _____	2. lotion _____	3. southerly _____
creek _____	loneliness _____	sorrow _____
crusty _____	locust _____	socialize _____
cringe _____	loaves _____	sometime _____
crock _____	loyalty _____	softening _____

Directions: Unscramble each sentence by writing the words in alphabetical order. Look at the second or third letters when words begin with the same letters.

1. caught fat eleven Carrie fish supper for

_____

2. Annie's midair in footballs Butch can bulldog catch

_____

3. through shiny several toes Todd's swam streaks silvery

_____

149

The **guide words** at the top of a dictionary page help you find entries quickly. The guide word on the left tells you the first entry word on the page. The guide word on the right tells you the last entry word on the page. The other entries on the page are between those two words in alphabetical order.

Directions: Write the number of the guide words that would be on the same dictionary page next to each entry word below.

1. belt/bind	_____	open
2. mine/moon	_____	stand
3. olive/ox	_____	moan
4. quack/quietly	_____	bend
5. stamp/star	_____	quick

1. back/bag	_____	basket
2. baseball/battle	_____	blink
3. beat/better	_____	badge
4. blanket/block	_____	bother
5. bonnet/bought	_____	begin

Directions: Read the guide words at the top of each column. Circle the one word in the column that would <u>not</u> be on the same dictionary page as those guide words.

1. **a/aid**
   afraid
   about
   ache
   also
   address

2. **each/east**
   easel
   eagle
   eat
   ear
   ease

3. **ladder/let**
   last
   list
   lead
   lamp
   leap

4. **dear/dish**
   deliver
   deep
   ditch
   destroy
   dimple

5. **imagine/increase**
   indeed
   immediately
   imitate
   include
   incident

6. **stage/storage**
   still
   steep
   stung
   stick
   stand

● The **respelling** that follows a dictionary entry shows how to pronounce that word. Use the dictionary's pronunciation key to help you pronounce each respelling.

Directions: Look at the full pronunciation key. Then follow the directions below.

a	hat, cap	j	jam, enjoy	u	cup, butter
ā	age, face	k	kind, seek	ù	full, put
ä	father, far	l	land, coal	ü	rule, move
ã	care, air	m	me, am		
b	bad, rob	n	no, in	v	very, save
ch	child, much	ng	long, bring	w	will, woman
d	did, red			y	young, yet
		o	hot, rock	z	zero, breeze
e	let, best	ō	open, go	zh	measure, seizure
ē	equal, be	ô	order, all		
ėr	term, learn	oi	oil, voice	ə	represents:
		ou	house, out		a in about
f	fat, if				e in taken
g	go, bag	p	paper, cup		i in pencil
h	he, how	r	run, try		o in lemon
		s	say, yes		u in circus
i	it, pin	sh	she, rush		
ī	ice, five	t	tell, it		
		th	thin, both		
		ŦH	then, smooth		

Directions: Read the respellings below. Notice the symbols in dark print. Beside each respelling write the words from the pronunciation key that show how to pronounce that symbol. Then write the entry word for each respelling. The first one is done for you.

1. l**ē**f   *equal, be* _____   *leaf* _____

2. r**ou**nd _____   _____

3. **ŦH**ose _____   _____

4. b**e**rn _____   _____

5. k**oi**l _____   _____

6. t**ü**l _____   _____

7. s**ô**rs _____   _____

8. n**ü**z _____   _____

9. **o**ks _____   _____

10. th**ã**r _____   _____

151

● When a word has two or more syllables, one syllable is stressed, or accented, more than any other. In the dictionary, an accent mark (') shows the syllable that is said with more stress.

Directions: Use the pronunciation key on page 151 and accent marks to say each respelling below. Then circle the syllable that is said with more stress.

1. rēd'ing
2. trub'əl
3. man'ij ər
4. mem'ər ē
5. ri välv'
6. ₮Hãr with'
7. dis tėrb'
8. bil'dər
9. un luk'ē
10. ri fresh'mənt
11. floun'dər
12. kə rir'

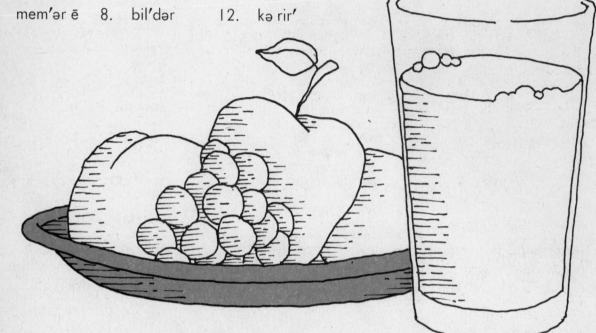

Directions: Use the pronunciation key on page 151 and accent marks to say each respelling below. Then circle the word in dark print that goes with that respelling.

1. sim'plē	**simmer**	**single**	**simply**
2. di zėrv'	**deserve**	**desert**	**dessert**
3. pas'chər	**pasture**	**patch**	**pastel**
4. ə slēp'	**assure**	**ashamed**	**asleep**
5. baj	**bug**	**badge**	**bus**
6. ₮Hėr'ō	**thereon**	**thought**	**thorough**
7. jin'jər	**jungle**	**ginger**	**garage**
8. ik splō'zhən	**explain**	**exploring**	**explosion**
9. süt'ə bəl	**suited**	**suite**	**suitable**
10. ga₮H'ər ing	**gathering**	**gardenia**	**getaway**

Remember, a pronunciation key shows you how to say words. A short pronunciation key may be found on each page with the entry words. Look closely at the pronunciation key below. Then follow the directions.

a	hat	ō	open	sh	she
ā	age	ô	order	th	thin
ä	far	oi	oil	ŦH	then
e	let	ou	out	zh	measure
ē	equal	u	cup		a in about
ėr	term	ù	put		e in taken
i	it	ü	rule	ə =	i in pencil
ī	ice	ch	child		o in lemon
o	hot	ng	long		u in circus

Directions: For each group, match each word in dark print with its respelling. Write the letter of the correct respelling beside the word. Use the pronunciation key and accent marks as a guide to say each respelling.

_____ 1. **anchor**   a. pri zėrv′

_____ 2. **preserve**   b. jü′əl

_____ 3. **haunted**   c. drô ər

_____ 4. **drawer**   d. hônt′id

_____ 5. **jewel**   e. ang′kər

_____ 1. **second**   a. lik′wid

_____ 2. **liquid**   b. i nôr′məs

_____ 3. **enormous**   c. gėr′gl

_____ 4. **loosen**   d. lüs′n

_____ 5. **gurgle**   e. sek′ənd

Directions: Can you read the riddles below? Use the pronunciation key and the accent marks to say the respellings. Then write the words from each riddle on the line below it. The answer for each riddle is given to you.

1. Hwut pärt uv ā chik′ən iz ver′ē myü′zi kl?

   _____

   the drumsticks

2. Hwich plants hav an′ə ml nāms?

   _____

   dogwood, cattail, and horseradish

3. Hwen iz ā kúk krü əl?

   _____

   when he beats the cream and whips the eggs

153

● Entry words are often listed in the dictionary without suffixes such as **s, es, ed,** or **ing.** When you search for a word in the dictionary, look for the word without those suffixes.

Directions: Match each word in dark print with the entry word you would look for in the dictionary. Write the number of the word on the line in front of its entry word.

1. **rosebushes** _____ erase
2. **footraces** _____ dispense
3. **dispensing** _____ footrace
4. **knotted** _____ rosebush
5. **erasing** _____ knot

6. **relieved** _____ fly
7. **equipping** _____ ranger
8. **rangers** _____ knife
9. **flies** _____ equip
10. **knives** _____ relieve

Directions: Read the paragraph below. Notice the numbered words in dark print. On the lines below the paragraph, write each numbered word as you would find it as a dictionary entry word.

Among the earliest European **visitors** to North America was John Cabot. In 1497,
                                  1
Cabot **landed** in North America. He is **believed** to be the first European to set foot on
        2   3
North American soil since the Vikings, **hundreds** of years **earlier.** Cabot was in the
                                        4   5
service of the English king and **claimed** the entire
                                 6
eastern coast of North America for England.

1. _____
2. _____
3. _____
4. _____
5. _____
6. _____

Sometimes you may notice that a word has a small raised number to the right of it. This tells you that there is another word pronounced and spelled the same way, but has a completely different meaning or origin.

Directions: Read these entries. Then decide which word to use to complete each sentence below. Write the entry word and its number on the line in each sentence.

hatch¹ (hach) **v.** bring forth young from an egg or eggs. (The chicks may <u>hatch</u> tomorrow.)

hatch² (hach) **n.** opening in the floor, especially of a ship, through which objects are passed. (The cargo was loaded through the <u>hatch</u>.)

post¹ (pōst) **n.** piece of wood, iron, or similar material set up to support something. (A sign was nailed to the <u>post</u>.)

post² (pōst) **n.** place where a person, usually a soldier, is stationed or on duty. (The guard remained at her <u>post</u> for an hour.)

rank¹ (rangk) **n.** a row or line of people or things placed side by side. (Pat played with the <u>rank</u> of tin soldiers.)

rank² (rangk) **adj.** having a bad, strong smell or taste. (A <u>rank</u> odor came from the swamp.)

stall¹ (stôl) **n.** place in a stable where an animal is kept. (The trainer led the horse to its <u>stall</u>.)

stall² (stôl) **v.** delay, put off. (Don't <u>stall</u> to do your homework.)

tire¹ (tīr) **v.** become weary or exhausted. (The long hike could <u>tire</u> us out.)

tire² (tīr) **n.** band of rubber around a wheel. (The flat <u>tire</u> on the car made us late.)

1. It took almost an hour to set the _____ for the mailbox firmly into the ground.

2. This chemical has the _____ smell of rotten eggs.

3. I had the flu last week and still seem to _____ easily.

4. The other team tried to _____, but the officials told them to quit delaying the game.

5. We closed the _____ to keep rain water from coming below the ship's deck.

6. My brother served on an army _____ in Europe.

7. Cleaning my horse's _____ is one of my daily chores.

⬤ When there is more than one meaning for an entry word, the different meanings are numbered. The most commonly used meaning is usually listed first.

Directions: Read these dictionary entries. Then decide which meaning of a word is used in each sentence below. Write the correct word and its defintion number on the line in each sentence.

ball (bôl) **n. 1.** anything round; a sphere. **2.** game in which some kind of ball is thrown, kicked, or hit. **3.** in baseball, a pitch that is not a strike.

band (band) **n. 1.** thin strip of material for binding or trimming. **2.** a stripe. **3.** number of people joined together. **4.** group of musicians playing together.

interest (in′tər ist) **n. 1.** a feeling of wanting to know, do, own, or share in something. **2.** in business, a share in property or actions. **3.** money charged or owed for the use of money.

office (ôf′is) **n. 1.** position or job, particularly in public service. **2.** place where work is done.

1. The kitten curled itself up into a _____.

2. Tad's mother owns part _____ in a hardware store downtown.

3. In our city, the mayor's term of _____ is set at only two years.

4. I receive _____ on the money that I keep in my savings account.

5. This summer, the city's junior high school _____ will give concerts in the park each Wednesday night.

6. A _____ of gold satin decorated the trousers of the uniforms.

7. Thomas and I share an _____ in science.

8. My mom and dad work in the same _____, so they see each other while they are at work.

Directions: Now put your dictionary knowledge to work. Read these entries. Then follow the directions below.

contain (kən tān′) **v. 1.** have within itself; hold as contents; include (This book <u>contains</u> useful information.) **2.** control; hold back (I <u>contained</u> my anger.)
dominate (däm′ə nāt) **v. -nated, -nating**
  1. control or rule by strength or power
  2. rise high above; become taller or greater
efficient (ə fish′ənt) **adj.** able to produce the effect wanted without waste of time, energy, or other resources
mineral (min′ər əl) **n. 1.** any natural substance obtained by mining or quarrying such as coal and silver **2.** a substance that is neither plant nor animal
mint¹ (mint) **n.** a place where a government makes coins used for money **adj.** new; not used **v.** to make into coins

mint² (mint) **n. 1.** a plant having a pleasant smell whose leaves are used to add flavor **2.** a piece of candy tasting like mint
organize (ôr′gə nīz) **v. -ized, -izing 1.** put in working order; get together; arrange **2.** bring together in a labor union
region (rē′jən) **n. 1.** any large part of the earth's surface **2.** any place, space, or area **3.** any part of the body
tundra (tun′drə, tùn′drə) **n.** a vast, level, treeless plain in the arctic regions
zinc (zingk) **n.** a bluish-white metallic element used as a coating for iron and in making alloys

1. Circle each word below that would come before the word **dominate** in alphabetical order.

        door   dolly   dock   donkey
        dormitory   dodge   dot   double

2. Circle the guide words that would be on the same page as the word **region.**

        restful/return   react/rebus   reason/remnant

3. Write each word from the entries at the top having only one syllable.

    _____   _____

4. Write each entry word whose last syllable is the stressed syllable. _____

5. Complete the following sentence with one of the entry words from above. Write the correct word and the definition number on the line.

    As our family left the restaurant, we each took a tasty _____ from the bowl.

Directions: Write the number of the meaning of the word in dark print that is used in each sentence below.

_____ 1. The pine tree in our front yard has grown quickly, and it now **dominates** the view from the window.
_____ 2. Jody added **mint** flavoring to the cookie mixture.
_____ 3. I felt a sharp pain in the lower **region** of my back.
_____ 4. This weekend, I will try to **organize** my closet.

When you finish any piece of writing, always proofread what you have written. Read slowly and carefully. Try to find and correct any mistake or error you might have made. The dictionary is a helpful tool for proofreading. Use it to find spelling errors. Also use it to check difficult words or words whose meaning you are not sure of. The dictionary will help you use the correct word and also spell it correctly.

Directions: Suppose that the paragraphs below are part of a report you have just finished writing. Proofread the report. Circle each spelling mistake. Write the correction above each error. Use the dictionary entries on page 157 to check the words that are listed there.

Canada's Northern Rejin containes one of the world's largest and most valuable wilderness areas. It consists of two territories, the Yukon and the Northwest Territory, which have not yet been orgenized as provinces. The area stretches from the Great Lakes to the St. Lawrence River all the way to the Arctic.

The warmer, southern part of the Northern Region is dommniated by forests that support an important lumbering industry. To the north, the tundres supports only a few Native Americans. These people survive on a land that is frozen in winter and swampy in summer.

The area's greatest wealth comes from meneral deposits of uranium, gold, iron, zink, copper, and lead. Transportation systems now being built will enable people to reach these deposits for efficiend development of the area.

Definitions and Rules

The **vowels** are <u>a</u>, <u>i</u>, <u>u</u>, <u>o</u>, <u>e</u>, and sometimes <u>y</u> and <u>w</u>.

The **consonants** are the remaining letters and usually <u>y</u> and <u>w</u>.

A **consonant blend** consists of two or more consonants sounded together in such a way that each is heard—**black, train, cry, swim, spring.**

A **consonant digraph** consists of two consonants that together represent one sound—**when, thin, this, church, sheep, pack, know, write.**

Short-Vowel Rule: If a word or syllable has only one vowel and it comes at the beginning or between two consonants, the vowel usually stands for a short sound—**am, is, bag, fox.**

Long-Vowel Rule I: If a one-part word or syllable has two vowels, the first vowel usually stands for a long sound and the second is silent—**rain, kite, cane, jeep.**

Long-Vowel Rule II: If a word or syllable has one vowel and it comes at the end of the word or syllable, the vowel usually stands for a long sound—**we, go, cupid, pony.**

Y As a Vowel Rule:
1) If <u>Y</u> is the only vowel at the end of a one-syllable word, <u>Y</u> has the sound of long I—**fly, try, by.**
2) If <u>Y</u> is the only vowel at the end of a word of more than one syllable, <u>Y</u> usually has a sound almost like long E—**silly, funny, baby.**

A **vowel digraph** is a double vowel that does not follow Long-Vowel Rule I—**school, book, bread, auto, yawn, eight.**

A **diphthong** consists of two vowels blended together to form a compound speech sound—**cloud, oil, new.**

Soft C and G Rule: When **c** or **g** is followed by <u>e</u>, <u>i</u>, or <u>y</u>, it usually stands for a soft sound—**ice, city, change, gym.**

Design and project supervision: M&S&F, Cleveland, Ohio

Illustrations: Bruce Serenta

Photo Credits: 5, 37, 48, 70, Ken Mengay Photographic Illustrations; 7, Dr. John D. Cunningham; 17, CR Studio; 25, The Coleman Co.; 26, 28, Ward's Natural Science Establishment, Inc., Rochester, NY; 30, Tennessee Valley Authority; 42, Girl Scouts of U.S. of America; 44, Courtesy of International Museum of Photography at George Eastman House; 46, 62, Gaines Dog Care Center; 55, U.S. Fish & Wildlife Service/photo by Don Livingston; 67, Buffalo and Erie County Public Library; 79, Photo by Jeffrey J. Loiko; 82, Comparative Sedimentology Laboratory, Rosenstiel School of Marine & Atmospheric Science, University of Miami, Miami, Florida; 92, U.S. Environmental Protection Agency; 95, NASA; 121, Ray W. Jones; 129, U.S. Fish & Wildlife Service/photo by Peter J. Van Huizer; 146, New York Convention & Visitors Bureau; 155, © Tom McGuire; 156, Carmine photo; 158, Canadian Consulate General: Tourism.

Definitions and Rules

To make a noun show **possession**:
1) Add **'s** to a singular noun
   dog's   Pat's   child's
2) Just add an **'** to a plural noun ending in **s**
   boys'   Browns'   babies'
3) Add **'s** to a plural noun not ending in **s**
   mice's   children's   women's

A **root** is a word or a word part from which other words can be made.
   port   pel   aud

A **suffix** is a word part added in back of a root.
   prints   packing   liked

A **prefix** is a word part that is added in front of a root.
   reprint   unpack   dislike

A **compound word** is made up of two or more other words.
   mailbox   sailboat   nonetheless

To make a word mean more than one:
1) Usually add **s**.
   cats   dogs   kites

2) If a word ends in **x**, **z**, **ss**, **sh**, or **ch**, usually add **es**.
   foxes   dresses   peaches

3) If a word ends in **y** preceded by a consonant, change the **y** to **i** and add **es**.
   skies   fairies   babies

4) If a word ends in **f** or **fe**, usually change the **f** or **fe** to **v** and add **es**.
   wolves   leaves   elves

5) If a word ends in **o**, usually just add **s** to make the word plural. Some exceptions are made plural by adding **es**.
   potato-potatoes   tomato-tomatoes   hero-heroes

6) Some words change their vowel sound in the plural form.
   man-men   tooth-teeth   mouse-mice

To add other suffixes:
1) When a short-vowel word ends in a single consonant, usually double the consonant before adding a suffix that begins with a vowel.
   running   hummed   batter

2) When a word ends in silent **e**, drop the **e** before adding a suffix that begins with a vowel.
   baking   taped   latest

3) When a word ends in **y** preceded by a consonant, change the **y** to **i** before adding a suffix other than **ing**.
   funnier   ponies   trying

160